31 Days of Healing

A Devotional

Connecting You to Your Healing

T M Leszko

Merging Streams Media

mergingstreamsmedia.com

31 Days of Healing

A Devotional

Connecting You to Your Healing

Copyright © 2018 by T M Leszko

All rights reserved. No part of this book may be reproduced in any form without written permission from Merging Streams Media.

www.mergingstreamsmedia.com

ISBN: 978-0-9959520-4-1 book

ISBN: 978-0-9959520-5-8 electronic book

Unless otherwise identified, all Old Testament and New Testament Scripture quotations in this publication are taken from:

The Holy Bible, Berean Study Bible, BSB Copyright ©2016 by Bible Hub

Used by Permission.

All Rights Reserved Worldwide.

Dedication

To my Lord and Savior Jesus Christ, the most faithful friend anyone could ever hope to know.

To Maclane whose challenges early in life became the inspiration for this book.

Thanks to Gary Ethier for his editing help and feedback.

Once again, many thanks to my family; your help in every phase of this project is greatly appreciated.

Table of Contents

Introduction 7
The Devotional 13
Day 1 - The Willingness of God 14
Day 2 - Outranking Your Crisis with Faith 21
Day 3 - Collective Belief and Agreement in Prayer 28
Day 4 - You Say Come, and I Say Go 35
Day 5 - Faith Can Alter God's Plans 42
Day 6 - Faith Connection – Who Touched Who? 49
Day 7 - The Blind Who See with Eyes of Faith 56
Day 8 - Don't Let Other Voices Silence Your Faith 62
Day 9 - Breaking Through Mental Blockages 69
Day 10 - When God Offends Your Mind to Reveal Your Heart 77
Day 11 - Raising the Roof, Jesus' Style 86
Day 12 - The Prophecy that Was Nearing Fulfillment 94
Day 13 – Lazarus – Part 1 102
Day 14 – Lazarus – Part 2 109
Day 15 – Lazarus – Part 3 117
Day 16 - After Eighteen Years Her Sabbath Rest Had Come 124
Day 17 - A Withered Hand Is Healed 131

Day 18 - Jesus Elevates a Person's Value 137
Day 19 - The DNA of Jesus...............................144
Day 20 - A Man Born Blind Is Healed..............150
Day 21 - Double Prayer to Cure Double Vision 158
Day 22 - When Unbelief Is a Perversion...........165
Day 23 - And Jesus Healed Them All 173
Day 24 - One Funeral – Two Raised from the Dead...179
Day 25 - When It's the Wrong Time to be Lending Your Ear...185
Day 26 - Jesus Sends Out His Ministry Teams 192
Day 27 - Intercession in Action 201
Day 28 - Spare Change to Heaven's Riches 208
Day 29 - Paul's Bold Act of Faith.....................219
Day 30 - All Things Do Work Together for Those Who Love God 226
Day 31 - The Intercession of the Ministry........233
Supplemental Teaching 239
Faith – Part 1 240
Faith – Part 2 250
Faith – Part 3 261
Final Thoughts 278
About the Author...280

Introduction

When I first felt the inspiration to write this teaching devotional, it was to help the readers come to the realization that their faith could access the power of God. Whatever the circumstances you are facing and whatever your need, you have a gift from God within you that can meet the challenge and overcome it. For some, that gift may presently be lying dormant, while for others it may only need the inspiration to be released.

This book is designed to be a resource of encouragement for your faith as you deal with life's difficult challenges. Furthermore, it is to let you know that sicknesses, diseases or any other infirmities are not your fated lot in life. So be assured that God has an action plan for your deliverance and healing.

Paul the apostle wrote these words in his letter to the Christians in Rome, *"Faith comes by hearing, and hearing by the word of Christ" (Romans 10:17)*. He was teaching the church that what you believe is the by-product of what you have heard and received as truth. That belief will lead you to act upon what you have embraced in your heart as real and true. When Paul wrote "hearing" for the second time he was emphasizing that hearing words about God brings forth actions based upon your belief in God's Word. Faith is not just a noun describing a religion or a tenet of belief. Rather, biblical faith is the belief that what God has spoken through His Word is the truth. That truth forms the basis of belief, which then leads a person to act upon it.

The first premise that we need to believe is that Jesus views sickness as the enemy of God. As we read the Bible, we learn from Jesus that our faith in Him can release His power into any situation in our lives. Those words, spoken nearly two thousand years ago, provide the same seeds of hope for us today. Unfortunately, we tend to believe the Lord only cares about our spiritual well-being, but that is not the case. When we learn that Jesus spent so much of His ministry healing the sick and delivering the oppressed, it should give us an idea that His concern for our physical well-being is very important to Him. Our total well-being represents His heart for us and our loved ones. His love for humanity has never changed, for in the book of Hebrews we read, *"Jesus Christ is the same yesterday and today and forever"* (Hebrews 13:8).

In other words, nothing has changed in His heart for mankind and more specifically, whether you realize it or not, that means you! You are the beloved of God and your well-being matters to Him. As much as Jesus was moved with compassion to heal the hurting and afflicted when He walked this earth, He is moved with that same compassion for you today. Even though He now sits enthroned in His glory as the victorious Son of God, He is not far from you or your needs. As we start to believe that those truths are true for us in our day, it will foster those seeds of hope, and they will sprout to life. From that living hope, your miracle will become a reality. Jesus said, *"All things are possible to him who believes!"* (Mark 9:23). The realm of the miraculous was commonplace to Jesus, and He makes that world available to us through our belief in Him.

Each daily devotion in this book includes a Bible passage that will inspire and ignite your faith. As you read, you will notice that after many healing encounters, Jesus told the person being healed it was his/her faith that accessed the power of God. That is one of the key purposes of this writing.

Introduction

In the New Testament, Jesus left us many parables that spoke about what the kingdom of God is like and how we enter or access it. He did this to lay a foundation on the solid rock of His life whereby a believer could live a supernaturally, natural life. The Lord's goal was to leave you well-equipped in this troubled and fallen world to face every challenge successfully. He often used the imagery of seeds and farming to reveal what the world of faith is like because that illustration is timeless and still relevant. Furthermore, it is through that analogy of farming that God gives us a template for a perpetual, growing, spiritual garden of faith. From those crops, you will have something that is ready for picking whenever the need arises. Most certainly, your faith can get you to your healing but even that would only be telling you half of the story.

You will not only read of people who are commended by Jesus for their faith, but you will also see others accessing the Lord's power on behalf of a loved one by faith. It doesn't even end there, for you will read of the beauty and compassion of the Lord as He comes with tender mercy and heals those who have little or nothing to offer Him in the way of faith. Even then, we still see His manifest authority and power come to heal people who have nothing to offer Him except a faint plea.

To me, those testimonies are some of the most beautiful examples of the care and the lovingkindness of Jesus. People who have had their hopes dashed in a world that is given to unbelief are never far from His compassionate care. That is the person I want to show you. If I show you Jesus and His heart, you will see that the source of His power is love because God is love, and faith works by love.

When people see the passionate love of Jesus toward them with the eyes of their hearts, change is at the door. When they see all that He is and all that He continues to do, it unlocks the doors of their hearts and opens them up to hope. For if you can see Him as He truly is, then all things will be possible to you. No door will remain closed.

We will begin with 31 days of devotional readings from the scriptures that will show you the Lord's heart for mankind and more pointedly, His heart for you. Each day you do your devotions, look to identify where the faith is coming from. It will help you form a greater foundation for your faith. Then, in keeping with the two-fold purpose of the book, we will offer some teaching on how faith works, how it is activated and how it is maintained.

If you have been given this book because you are in need of healing or a miracle, our prayer team is believing with you that through these testimonies and words you read, you will experience a release of God's power in your life. As you read through the following devotions, personalize them to your situation. Enter the story as if you are a part of it and apply each lesson learned to your life. As you do this, I trust your seed of faith will bring you the harvest of healing you are seeking. In Jesus' name.

T M Leszko
January 2018

31 Days of Healing

The Devotional

Day 1

The Willingness of God

If you have ever wondered how God feels about the health of a person and what His will is concerning healing, it is summed up in the following testimony.

Jesus Heals the Leper

> *When Jesus came down from the mountain, large crowds followed Him. Suddenly a leper came and knelt before Him, saying, "Lord, if You are willing, You can make me clean." Jesus reached out His hand and touched the man. "I am willing," He said, "be clean." And immediately his leprosy was cleansed. Then Jesus instructed him, "See that you don't tell anyone. But go, show yourself to the priest and offer the gift prescribed by Moses, as a testimony to them"* (Matthew 8:1-4).

So many things run through our minds when a health crisis arises in our lives or with one of our loved ones. Why did this happen? What caused it? Or who is responsible? We try to walk through the minutia of every detail trying to locate the source and cause of the affliction. We search the Internet looking for clues and rely on doctors, as well as specialists to hone in on the problem. We hope they can come up with the answers and cure. We even question God about why it happened. We worry that it may be some form of judgment and question whether He loves us or not; the list goes on and on.

The man in the above passage not only had a skin condition, but it was also the worst kind with no hope of a cure. Leprosy was a dreaded disease; the one most feared by the people in the first century because there was no history of anyone recovering from it in over 800 years. Naaman the Syrian was the last recorded case in Israel. As it relates to this man, he was not experiencing the onset of leprosy or had a partial manifestation of the disease; it was far worse. In Luke's Gospel account, we learn that he had a full-blown infection, which completely covered his face and body.

To make matters worse, the prevailing belief of people living in Israel in the first century was that leprosy was a sign you had sinned greatly against God and this was His judgment against you. Jesus had to constantly contend with that type of belief. He had to speak against it to help people overcome that mindset and get them on their path to healing.

One of the first sermons Jesus preached came from the book of Isaiah, which foretold what the ministry of the Messiah would be like. Jesus proclaimed His calling in the synagogues and quote this passage from Scripture,

> *The Spirit of the Sovereign Lord is on me, because the Lord has anointed me to proclaim good news to the poor. He has sent me to bind up the brokenhearted, to proclaim freedom for the captives and release from darkness for the prisoners, to proclaim the year of the Lord's favor* (Isaiah 61:1, 2a).

Jesus told all who would hear Him speak that He was the fulfillment of those words. He came to declare good news to the people that the time of their suffering was over. It was not a time of judgment, but rather, it was a time of great favor and blessing. It was not a day of favor as in short visitation; it was now a year of divine favor showing forth the goodness and kindness of God for an entire age. Every captive of soul or body was to be freed from his or her heartbreak and pain. Every lack, physically, emotionally, financially or any other thing that would cause a person to feel impoverished could be answered in Jesus. This was the Father's heart being expressed, not through the words of laws and judgment but through the compassion and love of His only begotten Son. Israel and the rest of the world would finally get to see what the Father was really like through the life of Jesus the Son, the Redeemer of the world.

So from this brief story, we learn of this dear broken man of soul and body who heard about the works of Jesus and sought Him out. From what must have been the faintest of hopes, something had come alive in his heart. When he learned that Jesus was nearby, he went right up to the Lord and knelt before Him in a bold and daring move. Lepers were never allowed to be anywhere in a public gathering. They had to shout out the words "unclean" to warn the people nearby that a leper was present.

That man laid all of his hope on the line and asked Jesus if He would be willing to heal him. He did not doubt that God could heal a person with a disease as horrible as his was; he just didn't know if God was willing to heal him. Before Jesus answered him, He reached out and touched him. That simple act said more to the man than a thousand words could have possibly conveyed. He probably could not even remember the last time he had felt the compassionate touch of another human. Now, he was receiving all of that and more because he was receiving a touch from God. The man's hope welled up into belief when Jesus told him He was willing; his healing took place in an instant. Jesus took the key called "I am willing," unlocked the prison door that held the man's healing and set him free.

Jesus could have spared Himself the uncomfortable experience of making physical contact with a leper by simply speaking a word of healing to the man. I am sure the man would have been overwhelmingly grateful, but the Lord was not just interested in healing him of his disease. He was interested in healing the man's soul as well. Taking the time to show the man kindness and love demonstrated to him that his life mattered. It restored some sense of dignity to the man before the healing took place.

Our beautiful Savior is not afraid to touch us in our uncleanness; no one is out of the reach of His touch. No matter what condition you find yourself in, you are always before a God who is not only willing to help you in your trouble but also cares for you deeply as a person. How beautiful is the Lord Jesus. He first restored the man's dignity and then his body.

How wonderful it must have been to witness the lovingkindness of God in action. As the joyful tears subsided, Jesus told the man to go to the priest for the required confirmation and pronouncement that he was clean of leprosy. This had to take place for the man to return to the life he once knew. In a way, it would be like a person in our day being healed and receiving confirmation of his clean bill of health from his doctor or specialist.

It is important for you to know that if Jesus was willing to heal that man, He is telling you through this testimony that He is also willing to heal you. Let your hope arise and be the platform of belief that launches your faith for the answer to your heart's cry. Believe that this is true for you or for your loved one because you are beloved of God. He is willing and is reaching out to touch you through these words. In what is known as the Lord's Prayer, we recite, *"Your will be done on earth as it is in heaven."* Well, I can assure you there are no sick or afflicted people in heaven, so if it is true there, it can be our reality here.

Prayer

Heavenly Father, I see in this story Your true heart and compassion for people in need. Help me to see You for who You really are. You are a loving Father and my life is held with great gentleness and care in Your tender embrace. Awaken trust in my heart; awaken the faith that moves any mountain I face and fulfill Your destiny in me. I ask and believe for my healing because I know You are willing. In Jesus' name, I offer this prayer.

Declaration

I know that I know that God loves me. He is willing and able to deliver me. I believe that healing is a gift of love from above, and I receive it into every fiber of my being. In Jesus' name. So be it!

> *For all the promises of God are "Yes" in Christ. And so through Him, our "Amen" is spoken to the glory of God* (2 Corinthians 1:20).

Day 2

Outranking Your Crisis with Faith

Faith in God and His Word is like being given officer status in the kingdom of God. It brings an endorsement to your words where your commands are actually followed.

Jesus Heals the Roman Centurion's Servant

> *When Jesus had entered Capernaum, a centurion came and pleaded with Him, "Lord, my servant lies at home, paralyzed and in terrible agony."*
> *"I will go and heal him," Jesus replied.*
> *The centurion answered, "Lord, I am not worthy to have You come under my roof. But just say the word, and my servant will be healed. For I myself am a man under authority, with soldiers under me. I tell one to go, and he goes; and another to come, and he comes. I tell my servant to do something, and he does it."*

When Jesus heard this, He marveled and said to those following Him, "Truly I tell you, I have not found anyone in Israel with such great faith.

Then Jesus said to the centurion, "Go! As you have believed, so will it be done for you." And his servant was healed at that very hour (Matthew 8:5-10, 13).

Soldiers Understand the Chain of Command

An army officer who was part of the occupying forces of the Roman Empire had been stationed in Israel for quite some time. During his time there, he had come to respect and honor the religion of this nation and even helped to finance the building of a synagogue. His servant had suffered a terrible injury that had left him paralyzed. In the first century, there was little medical aid to deal with the injury or the severe pain, which his servant suffered.

This officer heard the stories of the prophet healer named Jesus and went with a delegation to see the Lord. This man understood authority. He had one hundred men under his command and no order that came from his mouth would be disobeyed without dire repercussions, for that was the world of strict Roman military discipline. It was a world of authority and command from which, he knew the power of Rome backed his words and the orders he gave. When he heard about Jesus, he recognized that if people could be cured by Jesus' words, then He too must have authority and hold a high rank in His kingdom.

The big question of the day was if this Jesus was the Messiah, for most who believed in His ministry saw Him as a prophet or a teacher. In this centurion's mind, he surmised that whoever Jesus was, His position and the authority He wielded were highly ranked. Therefore, he felt unworthy that the Lord should come to his home. His only request to the Lord was His spoken command and that was the only thing needed for his servant to be healed and made whole. Just as he knew that the power of the empire of Rome stood behind his words as an officer, he understood that the power of God stood behind the Lord's words enforcing every order He gave.

What I find most striking in this passage is that the centurion recognizes Jesus' words had power and authority just as his had over the soldiers under his command or the slaves he owned. When he gave a command, it carried weight by the authority he wielded, and his soldiers and servants executed those orders. He acknowledged that Jesus had authority by His word alone to heal his suffering servant.

If soldiers and slaves fulfilled the command of this wealthy officer of Rome, then who is carrying out the Lord's commands? Could it be this is the function of the angels sent to minister on behalf of the heirs of salvation? Faith is the authority of command that releases God's creative power and commissions the angels of the Lord to act on our behalf.

> *Are not the angels ministering spirits, sent to serve those who will inherit salvation?* (Hebrews 1:14).

Like the enacted laws of a nation, angels are commissioned to respond to our prayers of faith in a similar way as the military and civil servants act to protect and preserve the laws of the land. When we act in agreement with God's will, our faith in God and His Word gives us entry into that realm of authority. It gives us the right to command and see the deployment of the resources and assets of the kingdom of God in response to our prayers of faith.

When Jesus heard this soldier's statement of belief, it is said that He marveled at such great faith. It was unlike anything He had witnessed in all of Israel and to top it off, this man was a Gentile. Certainly, he had little in comparison to the knowledge of God that even the casual believer in Israel would have understood. That should give us confidence that it is not by some great acquisition of knowledge that we gain faith but by simply believing and acting on what we know from the Lord.

> *And without faith it is impossible to please God, because anyone who approaches Him must believe that He exists and that He rewards those who earnestly seek Him (Hebrews 11:6).*

How delighted Jesus must have been that day to hear those words offered from the man with that kind of trust. That man would not be denied his reward. Jesus sent him home with the word of His command to affect healing and to cure his servant's body.

What makes this story even more interesting is that throughout Jesus' entire ministry, He stayed the course and proclaimed the good news of His kingdom to the Jews as His first priority. The job to spread the good news to the rest of the world, as well as Israel, would be given to His disciples. This man's faith had catapulted him into the New Covenant age that we currently live in. It was a future promise that would make salvation with all of its benefits available to everyone. That centurion brought it into his, here and now. It really wasn't his time to experience the good news of the Messiah, but his faith took him there.

The New Covenant is our time, so who will step forward and trust God as this centurion did on that day? Those who take the Lord at His word will not be disappointed; their faith will be rewarded.

Prayer

Lord, You told us to ask in prayer believing that we will receive whatever we ask for. Therefore, I ask for (state what you are believing for).__Thank You, Lord for answering my prayer. Like the centurion who took You at Your word, I do so also. Thank You for my breakthrough. In Jesus' name and in His authority, I pray. Amen.

Declaration

Lord, I believe You are true to Your Word. I believe You suffered that I could be healed. I declare that healing is my right and is the inheritance of all Your sons and daughters. I command every mountain and obstacle in my life to be removed, In Jesus' name.

Therefore, every sickness, disease or injury must obey my words that are backed by the Lord's authority and power.

> *Have faith in God," Jesus said to them. "Truly I tell you that if anyone says to this mountain, 'Be lifted up and thrown into the sea,' and has no doubt in his heart but believes that it will happen, it will be done for him. Therefore I tell you, whatever you ask in prayer, believe that you have received it, and it will be yours"* (Mark 11:22-24).

Day 3

Collective Belief and Agreement in Prayer

There is power in agreement and unity of purpose to accomplish the impossible.

Ten Lepers Healed

> *While Jesus was on His way to Jerusalem, He was passing between Samaria and Galilee. As He entered one of the villages, He was met by ten lepers. They stood at a distance and raised their voices, shouting, "Jesus, Master, have mercy on us!"*
> *When Jesus saw them, He said, "Go, show yourselves to the priests." And as they were on their way, they were cleansed.*
> *When one of them saw that he was healed, he came back, praising God in a loud voice. He fell facedown at Jesus' feet in thanksgiving to Him—and he was a Samaritan.*
> *"Were not all ten cleansed?" Jesus asked. "Where then are the other nine? Was no one found except this foreigner to return and give glory to*

God?" Then Jesus said to him, "Rise and go; your faith has made you well!" (Luke 17:11-19).

Ten men. Ten men with horrific deformations to their bodies and suffering of their souls. Ten men who lived with slow death sentences hanging over their heads.

Leprosy was a horrible disease that caused deformity and decomposition in the afflicted body with no hope of treatment and no known cure. It was considered to be highly contagious, which resulted in a person's removal from society and separation from all he or she held dear. Lepers were not to engage the public in any way and had to announce their presence with shouts of "unclean, unclean!" They were treated as outcasts; many thought they were better off dead. They were forbidden from getting close to prevent a "clean" person from the risk of breathing the same air as them. This was the state of these men who lived in caves or in colonies away from the towns and villages they once called home.

I wonder how many lepers heard the news about the miracles of Jesus in their isolated colonies. I wonder how many just sat there in their depression and suffering without taking any action for the chance of a changed life. Ten of these men heard that Jesus was nearby and determined that the hope of healing was worth the risk. They made the decision to seek Jesus as a group. If this was a scene on our streets where a group approached us with parts of their bodies already rotting and deformed, it might look like something from a zombie apocalypse movie. However, for the people of the ancient world, this was a true, horror reality. With all these factors against them, these men were not to be denied. They left with an agreed upon purpose and acted on their belief. Jesus was now in view, and they would never return to that colony again.

Jesus taught about the prayer of agreement when He said,

> *Again, I tell you truly that if two of you on the earth agree about anything you ask for, it will be done for you by My Father in heaven. For where two or three gather together in My name, there am I with them"* (Matthew 18:19, 20).

These men would not have known that they were acting in unity and agreement as Jesus had taught, but in a very literal way, this verse had come to pass. These Samaritans and Jews were united in their affliction. If they were whole and living a normal life, they wouldn't have had anything to do with each other. It is true that adversity brings people together and their "one voice" was an act of corporate intercession.

As they neared the village and saw the Lord, instead of shouting, "unclean, unclean," they shouted out, "Jesus, Master, have mercy on us!" These ten men were shouting at the top of their voices. Probably to the shock and horror of the crowds, these lepers had come too close to their town.

Jesus turned, saw them and without hesitation, yelled back at them to show themselves to the priest. That was all they needed to hear, just one sentence, but it meant everything in the world to them. They knew the first step to be welcomed back into their families and homes was to have the priest's pronouncement that they were cleansed of the disease. The priest's pronouncement of "clean" would be the same as getting your doctor's verification that you were, in fact, healed. Once they received that clearance, they could return to the life they once knew.

What is so striking about the faith of these ten men was that at the very hearing of the Lord's words, they acted and turned to go to the temple. They did not even stop to check themselves but acted on the words of Jesus without hesitation. These words coming from Jesus carried more weight to them than what their physical eyes could see. The Lord had instructed them to do something as if it had already happened. Clearly, it was not yet visible to the eye, but as they obeyed the word and went, the healing began to visibly manifest. Ten men were healed as they turned and departed; it was then that they saw the fruit of what they had believed.

Can you imagine their joyous outbursts as they looked at one another? Can you fathom how they felt when they saw each other's faces that were previously unrecognizable? Hopelessness, despair, broken hearts, destroyed lives, and leprosy were all healed by one instruction from the Lord.

Nine men went joyfully on their way, but one man turned back to thank and worship the Lord. Jesus told him that his faith saved him. Why was that the case? Salvation is found in no one other than Jesus. This man's worship of the Lord for his healing opened the doors of the kingdom of heaven to him. The others received their healing; however, this man received his healing and the promise of salvation.

Just like those men, you need to respond to God's Word even though you see no evidence of healing or feel any better. Acting on His Word engages your faith with His power. Faith will make anyone stand out in the crowd to catch God's attention, so take action in some way as those guys did. If you become a worshipper of God, you will stand out in the crowd as that man did. Be that guy!

Healing is a wonderful gift, but it cannot compare to having the gift of eternal life and being in good health. Your faith connects you to the God of the miraculous and because of His lovingkindness, His power is released. We ought to always remember this and live with gratitude in our hearts to Jesus our healer.

Prayer

Heavenly Father, awaken in me the hope and belief that You truly are my healer and that healing belongs to me. Stir my heart to act on that belief as those ten men did. Help me move in faith away from my situation and come directly to You as my answer. Thank You for hearing my prayer and for delivering me. In Jesus' name, I pray.

Declaration

Jesus, I declare myself to be "that guy" in the story. I believe in Your power to heal and deliver me from any affliction, and I receive my healing. I hear through Your words the answer of healing to my prayers of faith. I believe that You have made me whole. I worship and thank You for all You have done for me. Thank You again. You are my Lord and my God.

> *Truly, truly, I tell you, whoever believes in Me will also do the works that I am doing. He will do even greater things than these, because I am going to the Father. And I will do whatever you ask in My name, so that the Father may be glorified in the Son. If you ask Me anything in My name, I will do it* (John 14:12-14).

Day 4

You Say Come, and I Say Go

We must be open to the fact that the way we think things should unfold may not be the Lord's plan. But if we trust Him, we can come to the same good end we sought Him for through prayer.

Jesus Heals the Royal Official's Son

> *After two days, Jesus left for Galilee. Now He Himself had testified that a prophet has no honor in his own country. Yet when He arrived, the Galileans welcomed Him. They had seen all the great things He had done in Jerusalem at the feast, for they had gone there as well.*
> *So once again He came to Cana in Galilee, where He had turned the water into wine. And there was a royal official whose son lay sick at Capernaum. When he heard that Jesus had come from Judea to Galilee, he went and begged Him to come down and heal his son, who was about to die.*

> *Jesus said to him, "Unless you people see signs and wonders, you will never believe."*
> *"Sir," The official said, "come down before my child dies."*
> *"Go," said Jesus, "your son will live."*
> *The man believed the word that Jesus had given him and went on his way. While he was still on the way, his servants met him with the news that his boy was alive.*
> *So he inquired as to the hour when his son had recovered, and they told him, "The fever left him yesterday at the seventh hour."*
> *Then the father realized that this was the very hour in which Jesus had told him, "Your son will live." And he and all his household believed.*
> *This was now the second sign that Jesus performed after coming from Judea into Galilee* (John 4:43-54).

This family was facing a soul-wrenching situation as they watched their ailing son's condition worsen to the point of death. As a high-ranking government official during King Herod the tetrarch's rule, the very best medical treatment of their day was available to this man. They tried everything to help their child and every treatment known, but nothing worked. They had heard that there was a healing prophet in Galilee, and as a last resort, they decided it was worth giving it a shot by going to Him.

The town of Nazareth in Galilee was about forty miles away, and they just couldn't risk taking the boy on the trip. It was highly doubtful that he would have survived the journey. Hence, the goal was to go and bring the prophet back to their home in Capernaum. Now, no travel by land was quick in the first century. It would have taken a good part of a day to get there by horse, which was the fastest way or more than a day on foot. This was their last chance to save their son, so they left and sought Jesus knowing they had nothing else to lose.

Once they got to Nazareth, it wasn't hard to find the prophet named Jesus, for the locals told them to look for the crowds. People were coming from the surrounding villages bringing their sick and believing that their loved ones would be healed by a word or touch by Jesus. Sure enough, Jesus was easy to find. The official approached Him and pled with Him to come and pray for his son who was on the brink of death.

When Jesus began to speak, the dialogue took a very direct and focused turn toward the royal official. Jesus knew that time was running out for this family and so the Lord got right to the root of the problem. He abruptly told the man that unless he saw some sign or some great wonder from heaven, he wouldn't believe that God would heal his son. It was as if Jesus had read his mail and knew that his coming to Him was like taking a shot in the dark. So how would this dignitary react? Certainly, he was not used to being addressed in that way?

Sometimes, God will offend our minds to expose what we really believe in our hearts. Jesus, like a discerning physician, had diagnosed that the man was in fear and unbelief. The Lord would treat the man's condition first and then deal with his son's issue. On the surface, this would seem not to make any sense. But in reality, the man's belief was the core problem; therefore, it was necessary to draw out his faith like bringing up water from a well before the boy could be healed.

The man went to Jesus pleading, "Come, my child is dying," but Jesus told him, "Go, your son will live." Now, this man had to quickly deal with an internal conflict of soul. In his mind, he pictured the prophet doing something spectacular that would cause everyone to be in awe. Then they would see the boy healed and made whole. Instead, Jesus gave him the exact opposite of his plea, and it came with a single word of instruction: "Go." What was he supposed to say to his wife if he went home without the prophet? What if nothing had happened?

This is where the rubber meets the road for us all, or in this case, where the sandal or the horse's hoof meets the road. In the realm of faith, we have choices to make, and the actions that follow will dictate what we truly believe. Are we willing to lay down what we think is the right agenda? Will we surrender the way we believe things need to go? This is especially true when the action plan we are given is the exact opposite of what we think or believe. And finally, are we willing to trust that God truly has our best interest at heart? Or do we stubbornly insist it has to be the way we envision it to be?

This man had to make a choice that meant life or death for his child. He went to Nazareth with a word of instruction to Jesus: "Come." However, Jesus instructed him to "Go." There was no fanfare, no sign, and no wonder with the Lord's word. I am sure he was left to wonder if he was doing the right thing. He made a quick decision. By faith, he took the risk of believing the word Jesus gave him and followed the command to "Go."

During the long journey home, the official encountered one of his servants on the way. This servant sought to find him to deliver the greatest news this dad could have ever hoped to hear. His boy had completely recovered and was healed! After the absolute joy and elation subsided over the news, the royal official asked his servant what time the boy had recovered. He learned that it was the day before at the same time he acted on the Lord's word. When he returned and told everyone what had happened, a revival broke out among that family, as well as the servants and slaves; everyone became believers in Jesus that day.

There may be times in your life when the Lord wants you to act as the conduit of faith to connect a loved one to their needed miracle. I think it is safe to say, as it was for the father in this story that the faith of the parent or parents is vitally significant to the healing of the child. Nevertheless, whoever you are in relation to the person in need, the Lord is looking for you to be that "go to" person who can stand in the gap for the loved one in need. Release your faith, and act on your belief because – it's "go" time.

Prayer

Lord, I believe Your Word, and I will act on whatever You direct me to do. I lay down my thoughts, my own agendas, and any preconceived ideas. I will take up and do whatever You ask me to do. You have all the answers, and You are my answer. So I thank You right here and now for answering my prayer. I am not the sick; I am the healed. I also believe and ask that I be that conduit of faith for others in need. In Jesus' name, I pray.

Declaration

I believe that one word from the mouth of the Lord will release the miraculous in my life and the lives of others. Every sickness and disease must depart in the name of Jesus. Healing is my right and the right of every believer and their households. I also declare that my home is sickness and disease free, in Jesus' name!

> *He withdrew to a town called Bethsaida. But the crowds found out and followed Him. He welcomed them and spoke to them about the kingdom of God, and He healed those who needed healing* (Luke 9:10b, 11).

Day 5

Faith Can Alter God's Plans

In the last devotional, we read of a royal official asking Jesus to come, but instead, the Lord's instruction to the man was "Go." Every situation is tailored specifically by the Lord to release a person into his or her answered prayer. He does not use cookie cutter solutions on everyone but deals with each one of us individually. In this next devotion, the request is made to the Lord to come and He does. Let's find out why.

The Daughter of Jairus Is Raised From Her Deathbed

> *When Jesus had again crossed by boat to the other side, a large crowd gathered around Him beside the sea. A synagogue leader named Jairus arrived, and seeing Jesus, he fell at His feet and pleaded with Him urgently, "My little daughter is near death. Please come and place Your hands on her, so that she will be healed and live"* (Mark 5:21-23).
>
> *While He was still speaking, messengers from the house of Jairus*

arrived and said, "Your daughter is dead; why bother the Teacher anymore?"
But Jesus overheard their conversation and said to Jairus, "Do not be afraid; just believe." And He did not allow anyone to accompany Him except Peter, James, and John the brother of James. When they arrived at the house of Jairus, Jesus saw the commotion and the people weeping and wailing loudly. He went inside and asked, "Why all this commotion and weeping? The child is not dead, but asleep." And they laughed at Him.
After He had sent them all out, He took the child's father and mother and His own companions, and went in to see the child. Taking her by the hand, Jesus said, "Talitha koum!" which means, "Little girl, I say to you, get up!" Immediately the girl got up and
began to walk around. She was twelve years old, and at once they were overcome with astonishment. Then Jesus gave strict orders that no one should know about this, and He told them to give her something to eat (Mark 5:35-43).

In Mark's Gospel, we read of the synagogue leader named Jairus who went to Jesus in faith, believing that the Lord's touch would heal his daughter. That man's faith-filled statement moved Jesus to change His plans. Instead of going where He had planned, He followed Jairus to his home. When you take a moment to ponder what happened, it is staggering to the mind. A man's belief caused God to interrupt His plans and turn His attention to his specific need. Similar to what it says in Psalm 23, goodness and mercy followed Jairus to meet his child's need.

Faith in God and believing He is your answer to meet every need is like a homing beacon that draws the power of God straight toward your situation.

When Things Go from Bad to Worse

Throughout this man's encounter with Jesus, crowds were pressing in and around the Lord. Dramatic miracles had taken place all around them as they moved through the throng of people who were trying to reach out and touch the Lord. Jairus witnessed those miracles, and it must have bolstered his faith; he was going to need it. News had just come to him that his daughter had died, and there was now no need for Jesus to come.

Devastating news like that would crush any parent to the core of the soul, and I am sure it was no different for Jairus. Jesus overheard what was said to him and immediately stepped in to hold Jairus and whatever was left of his faith together. Jesus told him in a reassuring voice, "Do not be afraid; just believe." Those words kept hope alive in him; he and Jesus headed straight to his home.

By the time they arrived on the scene, the news had been heard in the community. Family, friends, and mourners had already made their way to the house. The loss of this young child was a tragedy and the cries that went up would have filled the neighborhood. Jesus took Peter, James, and John into the home of Jairus, for He could trust them to have faith in a traumatic situation such as this one. Jesus asked those in the house a question, for which He already knew the answer. So why did He do that? It was because He was quickly finding out if there was anyone with belief in that room. He then spoke a statement of faith, which was responded to with mocking laughter.

What Jesus was doing is what Paul described when he referenced Abraham's faith in God. For Abraham believed that it was,

> *God who gives life to the
> dead and calls into being
> what does not yet exist*
> (Romans 4:17b).

Jesus was speaking by faith in advance of what He was going to do. The next step that the Lord took was to get all of the unbelievers out of the house. Only the parents and His three disciples would experience what would come next. You see, as well-meaning, caring, and supportive as those family and friends were trying to be, their unbelief was poisoning the faith that Jesus was speaking into that room. It was only after everyone had left that Jesus went to the child and raised her from the dead.

Some important points are given through this awesome testimony of the power of God. The first is that faith attracts the attention of heaven. The second is when bad news is heard, we need to get a hold of our emotions, reject fear, and continue to believe. Fear is the exact opposite of faith, and unbelief is the opposite of belief. Unbelief and belief both work to form the thoughts that lead you to the actions of either faith or fear. Lastly, you don't need great numbers in prayer to see God move on your behalf. All you need are those who will truly believe with you in your prayer of faith.

If you should ever find yourself in a difficult crisis, remember the Lord's words: "Do not be afraid; just believe."

Prayer

Heavenly Father, I ask in Jesus' name that I would hear Your voice over and above every other voice. I ask You for faith that is an impenetrable shield, which absorbs the blows of every negative word. Give me discernment to recognize those individuals who will protect me in prayer with that same kind of faith. I trust You, Lord. Nothing is fatal or final until You have had the last say. You are the one I believe, and I thank You in advance for meeting my need. Amen.

Declaration

I declare that I will not be moved by any negative report concerning my health, healing or well-being. Jesus, I focus my thoughts on Your words to not fear but only believe. Your Word is the highest authority; it is greater and more powerful than any other word that is contrary to what You are saying to me through these scriptures.

Surely goodness and mercy will follow me all the days of

my life, and I will dwell in the house of the LORD forever (Psalm 23:6).

Day 6

Faith Connection – Who Touched Who?

Sandwiched in between the powerful account of the daughter of Jairus being raised from the dead is a powerful story of a woman's faith. With Jairus, it came down to Jesus touching his daughter. However, in this account, it's about a person touching Jesus. Her story provides a significant key to unlocking miracles in our lives.

The Woman with the Issue of Blood

> *And a woman was there who had been afflicted for twelve years by an issue of bleeding. She had suffered greatly under the care of many physicians and had spent all she had, but to no avail. Instead, her condition had only grown worse. When the woman heard about Jesus, she came up through the crowd behind Him and touched His cloak. For she kept saying, "If I only touch His clothes, I will be healed." At that instant, her bleeding stopped, and she sensed in her body that she was healed of her affliction.*

> *At once Jesus was aware that power had gone out from Him. Turning to the crowd, He asked, "Who touched My clothes?"*
> *His disciples answered, "You can see the crowd pressing in on You, and yet You ask, 'Who touched Me?'"*
> *But He kept looking around to see who had done this. Then the woman, knowing what had happened to her, came and fell down before Him trembling in fear, and she told Him the whole truth.*
> *"Daughter," said Jesus, "your faith has healed you; go in peace and be free of your affliction"* (Mark 5:25-34).

In the Gospels, we read of a woman who for twelve years had suffered from a continual bleeding condition. She had tried everything out there that claimed to be a cure. She spent everything she had on physicians and folk remedies in an attempt to get relief from her suffering and her condition, but it had only gotten worse. Nonetheless, things were about to change. She had heard about Jesus and all the wonderful healings that had happened through His ministry and now, He was back in town.

One can only imagine what this woman had gone through. The pain she felt and how weak she had become from the continual loss of blood must have been demoralizing. Yet, she was determined not to give in to her condition; she made a decision that would set her free. She was going to lay it all down on the line and get to Jesus. Her belief said, "If I could just touch the hem of His robe." That's all it would take to get her healing. It was time to put her belief into action. Her action became faith, and she and faith were on the move.

In Luke 17, the disciples were somewhat shocked after hearing Jesus teach on forgiveness. They were in disbelief as to how much forgiveness should be given to a person. It caused them to ask Jesus for more faith because the forgiveness and mercy they were required to give seemed to be too great a task for anyone to do. Jesus said two things in response to their request. The first was, no matter how small you think your faith is it has the potential to become large. The Lord used a tiny mustard seed as a mental picture to make this point. The second thing Jesus used to describe faith was the picture of a servant just doing his job. The servant Jesus described is one who doesn't expect praise and who will not rest until he has finished doing what he was commissioned to do.

A mustard seed doesn't have to figure out how to become a tree. It just grows in the right environment and becomes what it was designed to be from the DNA within that seed. A servant is given a chore and his master fully expects that servant to complete what he instructed him to do. So, in an ethereal sort of way, when you act on your belief, it is like a servant who carries out the believed instruction. Fears that are acted upon, work much the same way, so never employ fear under any circumstances.

That dear woman and her servant called faith, pressed through the crowd. She did exactly what she purposed in her heart and touched the garment Jesus was wearing. Immediately, she knew that a change had taken place in her body. Also immediately, Jesus felt a change in His body because the power of God had just been released from Him. With the crowds pressing in on Him, Jesus wanted to know who touched Him. When the disciples heard the Lord ask that question, they were probably saying in their minds, "Seriously? The crowds are all over you trying to touch you, and you want to know who touched you?" The woman knew it, and Jesus knew it, for faith had made the connection. So why her and not the others who were touching Jesus at that very same moment? Were they not trying to make that connection as well?

When you read the Gospels, you find that the people had mixed beliefs as to who this Jesus was. Some believed He was sent from God; others believed He was a deceiver, while others were unsure and wanted to see further signs as proof. Only God knew what was going on in the minds and hearts of those crowds pressing in to touch Jesus on that day. But one thing is for sure, if anyone else in the crowd had acted in faith, they would have enjoyed the same result the woman had. The message of her story is so important, we find it recorded in three of the four Gospels. It is a testimony of what can be your story and the rest of it can be His-story.

You may think that your situation is too big for your faith, but to Jesus, your faith can grow to meet every challenge in your life. Paul the apostle wrote,

> *Faith comes by hearing, and hearing by the word of Christ* (Romans 10:17b).

That is what you are doing by reading about God's power to heal through these scriptures. It is like water and sunshine to your seed of faith that has sprung up and is growing. Keep feeding your heart with God's Word and watch how grand your tree becomes. The problems will seem smaller, and your trust in God's power to meet your need will grow bigger with each passing day. It will continue to do so until you become fully persuaded of God's manifest power to complete His gift of healing in you. Press in towards Jesus and don't give up until the connection is complete.

Faith is contagious, and it can spread rapidly. In the verses below, we read of crowds of people touching the Lord, just as she did on the day of her breakthrough. Who knows, maybe it was her story that inspired these people to receive their healing. Determine to make your story of healing the catalyst for others to be healed and help others press through to Jesus.

> *When they had crossed over, they landed at Gennesaret. And when the men of that place recognized Jesus, they sent word to all the surrounding region. People brought all the sick to Him, and begged Him just to let them touch the fringe of His cloak. And all who touched Him were healed* (Matthew 14:34-36).

Prayer

Dear Lord, strengthen me to press in to touch You by faith just as the woman in the story did. Help me to move past the noise of the crowd and the obstacles that they sometimes become. Help me to not to hear unbelief or give myself to fears that would try to poison my faith with their words of doubt. Fill me with Your Spirit and empower me to total victory. In the authority of the name of Jesus, I pray. Amen.

Declaration

I will not stay in my current condition of need, for this is not my destiny. I will pursue You Lord Jesus, and I will touch You. I will see all that You have prepared for me and live to fulfill it all. This is my declaration. By these words, I set my faith as one who is engaged in your power. In Jesus' name!

> *And without faith it is impossible to please God, because anyone who approaches Him must believe that He exists and that He rewards those who earnestly seek Him* (Hebrews 11:6).

Day 7

The Blind Who See with Eyes of Faith

Deep within your spirit is the DNA of your heavenly Father. He created you in His image, which literally means that you were created with the characteristics of the living God. He has given you the authority to release His power through your words, which are rooted through your faith in Him. Two blind men came to experience the power that is released through believed and spoken words during their encounter with Jesus. Let's learn from their experiences and live out that same truth in every situation we may face.

Two Blind Men Receive Their Healing

> *As Jesus went on from there, two blind men followed Him, crying out, "Have mercy on us, Son of David!"*
> *After Jesus had entered the house, the blind men came to Him. "Do you believe that I am able to do this?" He asked.*
> *"Yes, Lord," they answered.*
> *Then He touched their eyes and said, "According to your faith will it be done to you." And their eyes were opened. Jesus warned them sternly, "See that no one finds out about this!" But they went out and spread*

the news about Him throughout the land (Matthew 9:27-31).

The Lord does things that on the surface might seem out of character by our estimations. But be assured that everything He does has our best interests at heart.

The two blind men in this passage of scripture learned that Jesus was coming by and cried out to Him; however, the Lord just kept on walking. These guys were blind; therefore, walking was a challenge even in the best of circumstances. Yet, they were trying to keep pace with the crowd and follow Jesus. So why did the Lord do this to these two men? Didn't He care about their situation?

Through the challenge that is presented and their demonstrated perseverance, the Lord would instill in these men what James wrote about in his epistle,

> *Consider it pure joy, my brothers, when you encounter trials of many kinds, because you know that the testing of your faith develops perseverance. Allow perseverance to finish its work, so that you may be mature and complete, not lacking anything* (James 1:2-4).

It would be a life lesson for them and to all who would read of the challenges those men overcame to receive their miracle. It would provide a foundation of faith that would serve them for all their days and give us a template of understanding for our lives. The Lord's goal was to bring their belief to maturity and by doing so, He gave them the key to answer any need that may arise in the future.

If those two men had quit trying to keep pace with the crowd and had become offended by the apparent insensitivity of the Lord, what would have been their outcome? They would have ended their days in blindness. Instead, they continued to pursue Him undeterred. As they groped their way in trying to keep pace with the Lord, they heard of others being healed. This would only serve to further enflame their hopes and rouse their faith even more. In their minds, they absolutely were not going to be denied.

When they finally stood before the Lord, He asked if they believed He could heal them. Jesus had already seen their tenacity. He already knew the answer to His question, but He wanted them to state what they believed. Why was this so? It is because His next words were not only going to affect those men for the rest of their lives, but they would impact everyone in the future who would read what Jesus purposed through this passage.

I Can, and I'll Use Your Faith

The Lord asked them if they believed He could open their eyes, and they answered with an unequivocal yes! The Lord did not tell them healing would come through His faith. Instead, He told them it would be according to their faith in His ability and power. He was telling the men that their faith can engage God's mighty power, no matter how great the challenge they are facing. Seriously, before Jesus came along, who in their day had witnessed a blind person receiving sight? Yet, these men did see the power of God both figuratively and literally. Figuratively, because they saw themselves being healed before it happened and literally, because it did, in fact, happen.

Jesus gave them the key to release God's power that would also sustain them in every future challenge they would face. Their persistence in pursuing Jesus beyond their emotional reasonings revealed they had faith that could overcome any difficulty or trial. They learned that they needed to act on their belief and declare that God is able to meet their needs. In doing so, their faith would engage God's power and release it into their lives.

Think about the challenges those two men faced as they pressed through those crowds to get to Jesus. The religious belief of their day declared that they must have been sinners; therefore, their blindness was a judgment from God. There was no social support system for them, which probably meant they were impoverished and lived on the streets. These men pressed through every emotional and physical obstacle that was before them to get to see Jesus; that is precisely what happened.

> *And without faith it is impossible to please God, because anyone who approaches Him must believe that He exists and that He rewards those who earnestly seek Him* (Hebrews 11:6).

Those men earnestly sought the Lord, and they tapped into the power of God through their tenacity; it led to their faith being rewarded. This example in Scripture shows us that through the perseverance of faith, we too can receive answers to our every need, just as those men did.

Never give up, and never give in to those obstacles you are facing. They may very well be the last line of resistance to overcome what will take you to your miracle. Residing in you right now is the faith that can tap into the power of God and give you everything you need to win the battle. So when you hear Him ask you, "Do you believe I am able to do this?" You know what the right answer is, "Yes Lord!"

Prayer

Father, I thank You that You are a God who is willing and able to answer my heart's cry to You. Nothing is impossible to You and no prayer request is too great that it cannot be met by Your mighty power. I am so deeply loved by You that nothing escapes Your heart of care for my well-being. Therefore, I ask You for (state your prayer request). I know You are faithful to answer my prayers and believe that they are granted. In Jesus' name.

Declaration

I am the beloved of God, and it's His good pleasure to manifest the power of His reign and rule on my behalf. Therefore, I declare my body is made whole in the name of Jesus. Every virus, disease, and malfunction in my body is brought into the healing power of my Lord and the divine order in which You created my body to function. Every attack against my health ceases in Jesus' name, and I declare myself completely made well. Amen.

I lift up my eyes to the hills.
From where does my help come?
My help comes from the LORD, the Maker of heaven and earth.
He will not allow your foot to slip; your Protector will not slumber (Psalm 121:1-3).

Day 8

Don't Let Other Voices Silence Your Voice

In the previous account, we read of two blind men following Jesus calling Him the Son of David to get His attention. They were acknowledging to the Lord that they saw Him as their Messiah. In this encounter with a blind man, he too acknowledges that Jesus is the Christ of God. The Lord stops and brings the man to Him. The Lord knows what the key is to unlock the door of healing for each person. Rest assured, He knows the key to yours, and there is no door He can't open.

Jesus Heals a Blind Beggar

> *As he drew near to Jericho, a blind man was sitting by the roadside begging. And hearing a crowd going by, he inquired what this meant. They told him, "Jesus of Nazareth is passing by." And he cried out, "Jesus, Son of David, have mercy on me!" And those who were in front rebuked him, telling him to be silent. But he cried out all the more, "Son of David, have mercy on me!" And*

> *Jesus stopped and commanded him to be brought to him. And when he came near, he asked him, "What do you want me to do for you?" He said, "Lord, let me recover my sight." And Jesus said to him, "Recover your sight; your faith has made you well." And immediately he recovered his sight and followed him, glorifying God. And all the people, when they saw it, gave praise to God* (Luke 18:35-43).

It is increasingly clear to me as I write about these wonderful accounts of healing, that they are all tailored by the Lord to meet the needs of each individual. In the book of Psalms, we read that we are fearfully and wonderfully made. He uses no cookie cutter solutions on you because you were never cut that way when He formed you in your mother's womb. You are a one-of-a-kind creation, and He knows what must be done for you to enter your miracle.

In this man's story, we read that because of his blindness, his life was reduced to sitting all day by the side of the road asking for alms. A beggar would try to locate himself where there was a steady stream of traffic, which would improve his chances of receiving some act of charity that might come his way. Unfortunately, in the first century, there were no support networks in place for those who were physically challenged, so begging was a way for many to eke out an existence. Sadly, they may have had to beg in an area where they had to compete with other people facing the same challenges to survive.

As we enter this story, we read that another day had come, and this blind man set out to follow his usual routine. He made his way to his familiar location. Once there, he listened for the sound of passers-by and made his plea as they neared. Unbeknownst to him, his life was about to be changed forever by an encounter with Jesus. This was not going to be just another one of those days.

In the region of Galilee, everyone had heard about Jesus and the miracles that took place through His ministry. They were all trying to figure out who He really was; that was the big question of the day. There was nowhere Jesus could go without drawing a large crowd of people, and that day was no different. As the Lord was moving down the road, the blind man heard the commotion taking place and asked some of the passers-by what all of the fuss was about. The people told him that Jesus of Nazareth was coming by. Speaking of Jesus as the one from Nazareth meant many things to many people. It was a term used to differentiate

Him from others named Jesus; it was a common name in the day. For others, it meant a prophet or a healer. But when Bartimaeus cried out to Jesus, he called Him Son of David and that separated him from most of the crowd. He was calling Jesus the Messiah and that got the Lord's attention. Though he was blind, he had proven through his belief that he truly could see.

He began yelling so loudly that people started telling him to shut up. Well, that just made him yell louder so that his voice could be heard above the din of the crowd. That man acknowledged what few were willing to when he cried out, "Son of David, have mercy on me!" He was stating for all to hear that he believed Jesus was the Messiah. His expression of his explicit belief brought the Lord to a complete stop. The Lord set His eyes on the man and had him brought over to where He was. He asked him the obvious question: "What do you want?" to hear the declaration of the man's faith.

Jesus had been teaching the crowds,

> *Ask and it will be given to you; seek and you will find; knock and the door will be opened to you. For everyone who asks receives; he who seeks finds; and to him who knocks, the door will be opened.*

> *Which of you, if his son asks for bread, will give him a stone? Or if he asks for a fish, will give him a snake? So if you who are evil know how to give good gifts to your children, how much more will your Father in heaven give good things to those who ask Him!* (Matthew 7:7-11)

Whether or not the man heard the Lord preach that message we cannot say, but He boldly told the Lord that He wanted his sight back. Jesus told him that his faith gave him the answer that he came to Jesus for, and his sight was restored. What this man first saw by faith was realized in his body. He sought the Lord through his bold proclamation that Jesus is the Messiah and drew the attention of heaven that opened wide its doors to him. In Mark's Gospel, we read that after Bartimaeus made His request to Jesus, he was told, "Go, your faith has made you well." At that moment of the man's request and the Lord's answer, nothing visibly had happened. Both of them were conversing in the language of faith, and it was in response to the Lord's word, "Go" that the miracle took place.

What a wonderful Lord, and what a wonderful gift that man received on this day for the ages. This man's great step forward was that he believed Jesus was his Redeemer. He boldly declared this to be true even while the crowds were still wrestling with the question of if He was even a prophet. Believing on Jesus moved Bartimaeus to the front of line for entrance into the realm of His power, and it will be the same for any person who believes in the Lord.

Don't let the voices of others talk you out of your belief. Drown out those voices by calling out to the Lord even louder and make your request known to God. They say that the squeaky wheel gets the grease. Well then, squeak on sister; squeak on brother. It may be an irritation to those around you, but to God, your faith is a most pleasing sound in His ears.

Don't let the Lord pass you by. Shout out to Him with a heart of faith and the kingdom of God will stop for you.

Prayer

Lord, I ask You to quicken and make alive those truths that I have held or now hold in my heart. Awaken my faith to action and help me to cast down every doubt and contrary thought that would come against my belief for healing. Release Your manifest power in and through me. In Jesus' name, I pray.

Declaration

I believe and declare that all power and authority resides in Jesus the Son of God. No sickness, disease or injury has a greater voice than God's voice to me. There is no power greater than God's power, and I believe that my voice is heard in heaven. I am the healed and no longer the afflicted; everything that seemed lost is recovered. In Jesus' name. Thank You, Lord. I believe, praise, and glorify Your name!

> *I lift up my eyes to You, the One enthroned in heaven.*
> *As the eyes of servants look to the hand of their master, as the eyes of a maidservant look to the hand of her mistress, so our eyes are on the LORD our God until He shows us mercy* (Psalm 123:1-3).

Day 9

Breaking through Mental Blockages

Sometimes, in order to activate your faith, you have to repeal in your heart and mind the contrary beliefs you hold. Whether they are traditions of your culture or religious traditions of your faith, they may be the stumbling blocks that are in the way of your victory.

The Healing at the Pool of Bethesda

> *Some time later there was a feast of the Jews, and Jesus went up to Jerusalem.*
> *Now there is in Jerusalem near the Sheep Gate a pool with five covered colonnades, which in Aramaic is called Bethesda. On these walkways lay a great number of the sick, the blind, the lame, and the paralyzed. One man there had been an invalid for thirty-eight years. When Jesus saw him lying there and realized that he had spent a long time in this condition, He asked him, "Do you want to get well?"*

"Sir," the invalid replied, *"I have no one to help me into the pool when the water is stirred. While I am on my way, someone else goes in before me."*
Then Jesus told him, "Get up, pick up your mat, and walk."
Immediately the man was made well, and he picked up his mat and began to walk.
Now this happened on the Sabbath day, so the Jews said to the man who had been healed, "This is the Sabbath! It is unlawful for you to carry your mat."
But he answered, "The man who made me well told me,
'Pick up your mat and walk.'"
"Who is this man who told you to pick it up and walk?" they asked.
But the man who was healed did not know who it was, for Jesus had slipped away while the crowd was there.
Afterward, Jesus found the man at the temple and said to him, "See, you have been made well. Stop sinning, or something worse may happen to you."
And the man went away and told the Jews that it was Jesus who had made him well (John 5:1-15).

Change Your Thoughts to Change Your World

We find in this account, the story of a devout man who continually went to a place where people had gathered and experienced healings in the past. Jewish tradition had said that an angel had appeared at this pool and as the waters were moving, anyone who stepped into those waters while they were troubled would be healed.

The pool at Bethesda had become a destination for the afflicted and ailing. They would position themselves along the walkway, wait for any sign of disturbance in the water, enter it, and claim their healing. I suppose, in a way, it is no different today when people make their way to places that are credited with notable miracles such as Lourdes in France or going to a ministry in a given city with a pedigree of healings. People go to these places or meetings in the hope that they will have an encounter with God, and some certainly do.

This man had faith lying dormant within his heart in spite of the fact that he had his affliction for 38 years. He was convinced that if he could just get into those waters when they moved, he would be healed. In his mind, it was the only known hope for healing in Israel, so he was determined to be there. Faithfully, he was brought to that pool and faithfully, he waited for his chance to be healed. For that man and countless other people, places such as Bethesda and Lourdes or a healing ministry become contact points that raise their levels of belief. Little did this man know that on that given day, he was going to have an encounter with the one who is the Healer.

Sometimes, we think we know the way God will or should answer our prayers. However, we need to keep our hearts open or else, we can miss it when the answer comes. This man's answer wasn't found in the troubling waters; it was found in the person of Jesus and in the response to His words. Out of all of the people who were lined up alongside that pool that day, Jesus sought that man. Faith is like a homing beacon that draws in the power of God, and it brought the Lord to him. That man had faith; it just needed to be realigned with the Lord's plan. That happened when Jesus initiated the conversation. The answer to the man's prayer was now standing in front of him.

What I find truly remarkable about this story is at that point, the man didn't have a clue who Jesus was and didn't even know His name. The Lord asked the man the most blatantly obvious question one could ask when he said, "Do you want to get well?" A question like that might have gotten a sarcastic response from someone like me who would have retorted, "What, do you think I'm just lying here poolside to improve my tan?" Jesus asked him that question because his answer would expose his heart and reveal what he believed. The man never answered the Lord's question with a "yes" or that he wanted to be healed. Instead, he told Jesus the problems he had trying to get into the water to be healed.

His answer stated that his circumstances prevented his healing from taking place. That was the key stumbling block to his belief, and it was keeping his faith in check. He believed he could be healed; that's why he kept going there. But in his mind, he needed some external help to get his healing. He had solved only half of his problem by getting to the place he believed he would find healing. The other half of the problem was finding someone who would sit with him day after day to put him in the water at that critical moment. He didn't have a faith problem; he had a logistical problem for which he had no answer. Therefore, it kept his faith from being activated and released.

Let Faith Arise and the Body Will Follow

When Jesus responded to the man's statement, He didn't ignore his answer.

Actually, He spoke to the answer by telling the man to "Get up." He shocked the man into moving out of his own prison of preconceived notions and spoke directly to his faith. In the same way that his body was lying dormant on the mat, so also was this man's faith. Those words from Jesus provoked action and as the man moved to obey the stranger's words, his body began to change; his healing took place immediately. That man with a heart full of thanksgiving and praise headed to the temple to worship the God who had healed him, not knowing that all the while, He was standing there right in front of him. It was only when he met Jesus again at the temple that he learned who Jesus was. His encounter ended with the Lord speaking into his life once more.

Religion will try to teach you to get your life right with God first and then He will heal you. But God, through His goodness and mercy, will heal you first and then speak into your life.

This story relates to us that sometimes we lie down and opine reasons we are not healed when Jesus is saying to us through His Word, "Get up!" Acting on His words unleashes the faith that He has placed in you. So rise and be healed. Remove every thought that suggests you can't be healed from your mind. Whether you believed a word from a doctor, family member, friend, a respected teacher, religious leader or from your own human reasonings, clear the slate of belief in your mind. Rid yourself of any thought that denies God's healing power from touching your life. Go to these Bible verses and passages and make them yours, for the power of God is released when you act on His Word.

Prayer

Lord, I lay down any preconceived ideas that I have harbored in my heart about healing or how healing may come to me. I look to You as the one who has the final say on the matter, and I place my trust in You. I ask You to unleash my faith as You did for that man in the story; let it destroy any sickness and disease that seeks to invade my body. Thank You, Lord for the love You have for me that is beyond my comprehension. I truly believe nothing is too hard for You. In Jesus' name, I pray. Amen.

Declaration

I declare that this body of mine is off limits to sickness and disease and that Your divine health preserves me safe and free of any virus or infection. Thank You, Lord that I will live out my days prospering and in good health even as my soul prospers. My every blessing is found in the knowledge of Your awesome goodness and with thanksgiving. I make this my statement of faith for every day of my life. Amen.

> *Bless the LORD, O my soul, and all that is within me, bless His holy name. Bless the LORD, O my soul, and do not forget all His kind deeds—He who forgives all your iniquities, and heals all your diseases, who redeems your life from the pit, and crowns you with loving devotion and compassion, who satisfies you with good things, so that your youth is renewed like the eagle's* (Psalm 103:1-5).

Day 10

When God Offends Your Mind to Reveal Your Heart

There is not a malicious bone in the body of Jesus – before His resurrection or after. He is neither uncaring nor insensitive to the pain of others. So, when it appears that way, there has to be an underlying purpose. Jesus is always looking to move a person to the answered prayer he or she is seeking.

The Healing of the Demonized Daughter

> *Leaving that place, Jesus withdrew to the district of Tyre and Sidon. And a Canaanite woman from that region came to Him, crying out, "Lord, Son of David, have mercy on me! My daughter is miserably possessed by a demon."*
> *But Jesus did not answer a word. So His disciples came and urged Him, "Send her away, for she keeps crying out after us."*
> *He answered, "I was sent only to the lost sheep of the house of Israel."*
> *The woman came and knelt before him. "Lord, help me!" she said.*

> *But Jesus replied, "It is not right to take the children's bread and toss it to the dogs." "Yes, Lord," she said, "even the dogs eat the crumbs that fall from their master's table."*
> *"O woman," Jesus answered, "your faith is great! Let it be done for you as you desire." And her daughter was healed from that very hour* (Matthew 15:21-28).

Healing Is the Children's Bread

Everything about the life and ministry of Jesus was laid out in advance in God's plan to redeem the world. Jesus literally had to walk back and reclaim all that was lost through Adam and then completely fulfill all of the requirements of righteousness under the Old Covenant. Nothing could be left undone in order for the Lord to usher in and establish the New Covenant, which is the good news of grace through faith in Jesus Christ. The successful completion of His mission would restore mankind to God's originally intended relationship and destiny. The challenge was daunting and Israel would be Priority # 1 in this step-by-step process. Once all of the legal requirements were met under the Law of Moses, Jesus could then bring the good news to the rest of the world through His disciples. That should provide you with a very basic overview of the dialogue that took place in this story.

Jesus was in a seemingly nonstop ministry mode with barely a chance to get some rest and recharge His batteries. So to take a breather, He crossed the border with His team of disciples and went to a place near the cities of Tyre and Sidon in what would be modern Lebanon today. They were possibly hoping for some anonymity in this Gentile region but that was not to be the case. The fame of Jesus had spread rapidly, even beyond the borders of Israel.

Almost immediately, as the word hit the streets, people began to seek Him. In those days, Jews were to have no personal contact with Gentiles. Hence, to speak to a foreign woman would have been utterly taboo and leading to a scandal. In the Roman world, everyone outside the rule and culture of Rome was considered barbarian. It placed you in a category of being something like a sub-human. In the Jewish world, anyone who was not a Jew was considered a Gentile, and they also were slandered as being sub-human – like dogs. The doors of cultural animosity swung both ways between the Jews and the Gentiles.

It is here that the story brings us to a woman who would have known about all of the aforementioned cultural stumbling blocks. Yet, she still sought the Jewish prophet. Her daughter was probably experiencing seizures, which in the ancient world was looked upon as demon possession. In this scripture passage, it indicates that what today would be seen as a physical and neurological malady was, in fact, caused by demonization. This made her desperate mother cry out to Jesus for help.

Along with this situation, we are brought into the midst of a first century socially uncomfortable situation. The woman came to Jesus addressing Him in Messianic language pleading with Him for her daughter's deliverance. The disciples wanted her to just go away, but they wanted Jesus to tell her to do so. However, all the while, Jesus remained silent. I am sure the disciples were rattling off all of the common reasons for her not to be there, but she was not to be denied.

People react differently when they find themselves in awkward situations, and it is exacerbated when it is met with silence. You tend to want to fill the void by saying something, but in this story, Jesus let the situation reveal what was in the heart of everyone involved. If Jesus had told her to go away, not a single person in the crowd would have thought anything by it; that's just the way it was in those days. Instead, Jesus turned and spoke with her, which was something that Jews just would not have done. He answered her from the paradigm that a Jew and a Gentile of that day would have understood.

She had called Jesus the Son of David, which was her acknowledgment that He is the Messiah. Did she believe this or was this just another kick at the can by calling out to anybody who could remedy her daughter's torment? The Lord's first response is the truth concerning His mission to the lost of Israel. I can imagine a scenario that the Lord, in keeping with His Israel first mandate, would have later answered this woman's plea. He could have easily instructed His disciples to search for her and deliver her child after He ascended. However, faith can move God to make other plans and that is why your trust in Him is so powerful.

The second statement Jesus made is that she was a Gentile (a dog) and the bread that He was serving was for the healing of Israel. She heard what He first said; yet, she continued to intercede for her child. When she heard the Lord using parabolic language in His second response, she turned His parable on Him by saying that even the dogs got something at the master's table. If this was a tennis match, she would have just crushed what the Lord served to win the point, and Jesus loved it.

It is astounding that a person's faith can even supersede divine order. It moves you to the forefront of God's passion like a hot knife through butter. She endured insult, refused to be offended, and did not let the Lord off the hook until she got what she went for. That is tenacious faith, and it is well pleasing to the Lord.

Jesus was blown away by her great faith and marveled at her tenacity. He no longer referred to her in the derogatory name for a Gentile because her faith in Jesus transcended nationalities and gave her entrance into the kingdom of God. She was an, "O woman," one who was admired by Jesus and who stood out from the crowd. Thus, she was given praise from the Lord for her unrelenting trust in His goodness. She refused to accept no as an answer and for her steadfast faith, she received deliverance and healing for her daughter in that very hour. Many in Israel called Jesus the Son of David but really didn't believe it. This foreigner demonstrated her faith in Jesus through her words and by her actions. She was unwavering in her belief that the Son of God was merciful and good. Neither silence nor insult was going to change her mind.

If I were the public relations director for Jesus' ministry responsible for getting His biography ready for publication, this story would not be used. I would probably say to Him, "Couldn't we use one of the thousands of other testimonies of healing and deliverance for your biography instead of this one? Let's use a story that paints you in a better light and not use this one at all." Jesus did not only make sure that this woman's story was recorded for all posterity, but He also had her story recorded twice in the Gospels. Jesus bestowed on this woman double honor for her outstanding faith and wanted this to be a memorial to her. Not only that, her example of faith was a great teaching lesson for all who would read and learn from her testimony.

In those times of difficulty when God seems silent, you must keep pressing into Him. Even when you may be judged as being unworthy of His healing, you must ignore those thoughts and keep pressing into the Lord. Use His words as the ground that you stand upon when making your appeal. Be steadfast in your faith that His Word and truth applies to you and your situation. If you do, you can expect no less than what the Canaanite woman received. You too may find yourself in the Lord's Faith Hall of Fame.

Prayer

Dear Father, I ask You for the strength and the perseverance that this woman had in her life. Awaken my faith by whatever means necessary that I will be one who can't be denied and the one who never ceases to pursue You. All that I need is found in You. Show me how to draw from Your well of provision today. In Jesus' name. Amen.

Declaration

I believe with all of my heart that God is my provision and the Lord is the answer to my every need. I will not be denied. Silence will not stop me. Others will not turn me away, and I refuse to be offended. I declare that God has heard my cry, and He has answered me with His kindness and favor. I believe this to be true, and in Jesus' name, I make this declaration.

> *Therefore, since we have such a great high priest who has passed through the heavens, Jesus the Son of God, let us hold firmly to what we profess. For we do not have a high priest who is unable to sympathize with our weaknesses, but we have one who was tempted in every way that we are, yet was without sin. Let us then approach the throne of grace with confidence, so that we may*

receive mercy and find grace to help us in our time of need (Hebrews 4:14-16).

Day 11

Raising the Roof, Jesus' Style

Intercessors are those who stand in the gap petitioning God on behalf of man. This story is a testimony of friends who acted on behalf of a friend. This is the spirit and heart of the intercessor; they are the ones who press in for others with a boldness of faith.

Jesus Heals a Paralytic

> *One day Jesus was teaching, and the Pharisees and teachers of the law were sitting there. People had come from Jerusalem and from every village of Galilee and Judea, and the power of the Lord was present for Him to heal the sick.*
> *Just then, some men came carrying a paralyzed man on a mat. They tried to bring him inside to set him before Jesus, but they could not find a way through the crowd. So they went up on the roof and lowered him on his mat through the tiles into the middle of the crowd, right in front of Jesus. When Jesus saw their faith, He said, "Friend, your sins are forgiven."*

> *But the scribes and Pharisees began to consider this and ask, "Who is this man who speaks blasphemy? Who can forgive sins but God alone?"*
> *Knowing what they were thinking, Jesus replied, "Why do you question this in your hearts? Which is easier: to say, 'Your sins are forgiven,' or to say, 'Get up and walk?' But so that you may know that the Son of Man has authority on the earth to forgive sins..." He said to the paralytic, "I tell you, get up, pick up your mat, and go home."*
> *Immediately the man stood up before them, took what he had been lying on, and went home glorifying God. Everyone was taken with amazement and glorified God. They were filled with awe and said, "We have seen remarkable things today"*
> (Luke 5:17-25).

Whenever a story is repeated in the Gospels, it signals to me that what is being reported is significant for the reader to know and understand. In the Gospels of Matthew, Mark, and Luke, we read the story of the healing of a paralyzed man and how it occurred.

At an early stage of His ministry, Jesus went to His own hometown, possibly for a short rest. He was possibly staying at His family's home while He was in town and it did not take long before the crowds began to gather outside the door.

The news had spread about Jesus throughout Israel, and religious leaders were now coming from Jerusalem trying to figure out what was going on with this Jesus and who exactly was this miracle worker. It makes you wonder how thrilled the owner of the house where Jesus was staying felt about the commotion taking place outside. As the crowd grew at the front door, Jesus wasted no time. Immediately, He began to minister to the people. They came to hear His words, see His works, and to be healed of their afflictions. In an age where there was no such thing as a medical center and so little known about health and healing, Jesus was like a living mobile hospital. It didn't matter how tired He felt, His compassion for the people would not allow Him to turn anyone away.

Appearing on the scene were some men with their paralyzed friend whom they carried into town on something that could be described as a stretcher. The crowd was so large that they couldn't get anywhere near Jesus, so they decided they would find another way. One of them had the idea to get in through the tiles on the roof. A typical home in Israel was a one-story building with a flat roof that was supported by crossbeams. Dried branches would be laid across those beams, which were then covered with straw or other organic material. It was built strong enough to be used as an upper, outdoor living space that the family could use. This kind of roof construction enabled the men to open a section of the roof tiles and lower their friend into the house.

You had to know those guys were absolutely certain this was not going to be a wasted exercise. They were convinced that their friend would be healed and were willing to offer their time and expense to repair any damage they would cause. Faith always gets the attention of Jesus, and the actions of those men certainly got the Lord's. They had charged the atmosphere with faith and now Jesus would speak into their friend's life to get him positioned spiritually for his healing breakthrough. One breakthrough of a roof would result in a breakthrough in the life of their friend.

Breaking the Power of Unbelief

As we examine the Lord's ministry, we notice that He creates a shift in a person's beliefs to awaken faith in a person's heart.

With that in mind, the first thing Jesus told the man was that his sins were forgiven. What this man believed about himself must have been the key roadblock to his belief that he could be healed. Jesus got that stumbling block out of the way so that the man's faith could be released. Of course, this upset all the religious people in the room because they didn't really believe in Jesus anyway and were offended that He was forgiving sins.

Throughout these devotions, you will read of the widespread belief, which taught that people who were afflicted were in that state because they were under the judgment of God. This would be the main blockage for most people to overcome and receive their healing. After all, if they believe God put sickness and disease on them, why should they ever believe that they should recover or receive healing from Him?

When someone is paralyzed, the instructions from the brain are not being transferred through the nervous system, which would normally trigger that particular body part to move. There is a disconnection in the system; something is broken. Unbelief works in the same way as paralysis. It interrupts or halts the belief from transforming into faith, which moves a person to action. When Jesus told the man to take heart in the knowledge that his sins were forgiven, He used that key to unlock in that man, the same faith that was expressed through his friends. That led to all of them being of the same heart and mind, which released the miracle as the end result.

What held down this man's faith was that he believed he deserved this judgment of affliction on his life. Whether that was told to him by some religious leader, or he was crippled by the weight of his own self-condemnation for his sin, we do not know. However, the pattern of crippling unbelief was broken by the truth from Jesus and the path to his healing was now cleared.

The cross of Christ has done the same thing for every man, woman, and child. It speaks to us all that our sins are forgiven and that we can enter a new life that has been freely given to us from Jesus our Redeemer. Every person has this same open heaven to God as those men had to Jesus through the roof with their friend. Can you imagine the celebration that happened at that moment? The roof of that place probably came off again. That is what you can call, "Raising the Roof, Jesus' Style."

The faith of others can help bring us to an encounter with Jesus. Such faith builds up hope. Nevertheless, we must respond to the

Lord with belief as our first step. The Lord slew the religious elephant in the room by telling the man that he was forgiven, thereby casting out that false belief for all to hear. By doing this, Jesus addressed the religious leaders in front of the paralytic man. They might very well have been the source of what he had believed about himself. It is only then that He told the man to rise, take up his bed, and walk. His obedience to the command of the Lord released the power of God, and his body was restored. The man's heart was beautifully prepped for belief by the words of Jesus, and he rose up healed in body and soul.

You might have great friends in your life who are determined to see you made well just like those guys in this account of healing. It might have been one of them who gave you this book to bring your thoughts to Jesus, your healer. Take the key Jesus gave that man and know God is not the one withholding you from your healing. Jesus forgave the sins of all mankind on the cross. Therefore, Like that man, we need to believe that is also true for us. Any religious belief or teaching that says you are somehow disqualified from God's healing touch is another elephant in the room that needs to be removed.

Prayer

Father, make this truth come alive in me, and let my faith be seen by You as a lighthouse beacon guiding me like a ship to your answered prayer. Lord, thank You for being the harbor for my soul and the port to anchor my heart in. Thank You for my healing. I believe it is mine. In Jesus' name. Amen.

Declaration

Jesus, You purchased my forgiveness and healing at the cross. Therefore, I declare myself free and released from any mental prison that would make me believe I deserve any sickness or disease. I recognize now that those are lies from hell to hold me in bondage and prevent me from enjoying all of the benefits of the free gift of salvation Jesus made possible for me. I declare myself healed and made entirely whole through Jesus Christ my Lord.

> *He Himself bore our sins in His body on the tree, so that we might die to sin and live to righteousness. "By His stripes you are healed"* (1 Peter 2:24).

Day 12

The Prophecy That Was Nearing Fulfillment

A prophecy concerning Jesus that had yet to be fulfilled had become the core message of the following testimony of healing.

Peter's Mother-in-law Healed

> *When Jesus arrived at Peter's house, He saw Peter's mother-in-law sick in bed with a fever. He touched her hand, and the fever left her, and she got up and began to serve them. When evening came, many who were demon-possessed were brought to Jesus, and He drove out the spirits with a word and healed all the sick. This was to fulfill what was spoken through the prophet Isaiah: "He took on our infirmities, and carried our diseases"* (Matthew 8:14-17).

It was a full day of ministry. Jesus and His disciples wanted to get some rest and maybe a bite to eat to end their day. Peter suggested they go to his home, but when they got there, they found that his mother-in-law had taken ill. She was stricken with a fever and was in bed. She was in no way able to host Jesus and His disciples. Sickness had entered Peter's home like an unwelcomed squatter, but it would have no chance to remain there in the presence of Jesus. Luke's Gospel records that Jesus rebuked the fever, took her hand, and she was made completely well.

They barely had time to finish their supper when crowds began showing up at Peter's door. There was no time for Jesus to get any rest because the people of the town had discovered where He was, and they brought their sick, afflicted, and oppressed for healing, as well as deliverance. That night, none of those people left the way they came, for they were all healed by Jesus' word and His touch. As wonderful as it is to read that everyone had been healed, was that the underlying message of this story?

Matthew was one of the Lord's disciples and the writer of this Gospel. At the end of his brief account of what took place on the day, he quoted a verse from the prophet Isaiah that was written some seven hundred years before the birth of Christ. What is unusual about this quote is the context in which it is taken. This passage was the prophetic description of the suffering the Messiah would endure in order to release the blessings of the New Covenant. Jesus took upon Himself the sins of the world, and they were nailed with Him to the cross. He bore in His body all of our infirmities and diseases with every lash of the whip that tore through His body. Every wound Jesus received paid the price for our healing and wholeness.

Matthew was speaking about an event that had not yet taken place. It was as if the Lord was paying in advance for these healings during His 3-year ministry with a post-dated check or bank guarantee on our behalf. That check would be cashed or the guarantee accessed through His suffering and death on the cross. What this further tells us is that everything the people experienced in their day concerning healing from Jesus is also applicable to us because it was part of His work of redemption for all mankind.

Israel, in the time of Jesus, had little concept of a suffering Messiah who was foretold by its prophets. They only believed in a coming, conquering Messiah who would deliver the nation from all its enemies and restore the kingdom to the glorious age of David's reign for all eternity. That is why they did not recognize Jesus. He did not fit their religious model. Yet, this passage from the book of Isaiah was hiding there in plain sight. He prophesied these words,

*Who has believed our message and
to whom has the arm of
the Lord been revealed?
He grew up before him like a tender
shoot, and like a root out of dry
ground.
He had no beauty or majesty to
attract us to him, nothing in his
appearance that we should desire
him.
He was despised and rejected by
mankind, a man of suffering, and
familiar with pain.
Like one from whom people hide
their faces he was despised, and we
held him in low esteem.
Surely he took up our pain and bore
our suffering, yet we considered him
punished by God, stricken by him,
and afflicted.
But he was pierced for our
transgressions, he was crushed for
our iniquities; the punishment that
brought us peace was on him, and by
his wounds we are healed.
We all, like sheep, have gone astray,
each of us has turned to our own
way; and the Lord has laid on him
the iniquity of us all.
He was oppressed and afflicted, yet
he did not open his mouth; he was
led like a lamb to the slaughter, and*

*as a sheep before its shearers is
silent, so he did not open his mouth.
By oppression and judgment he was
taken away.
Yet who of his generation protested?
For he was cut off from the land of
the living; for the transgression of
my people he was punished.
He was assigned a grave with the
wicked, and with the rich in his
death, though he had done no
violence, nor was any deceit in his
mouth.
Yet it was the Lord's will to crush
him and cause him to suffer, and
though the Lord makes his life an
offering for sin, he will see his
offspring and prolong his days, and
the will of the Lord will prosper in
his hand.
After he has suffered, he will see the
light of life and be satisfied; by his
knowledge my righteous servant will
justify many, and he will bear their
iniquities.
Therefore I will give him a portion
among the great, and he will divide
the spoils with the strong, because he
poured out his life unto death, and
was numbered with the
transgressors.*

> *For he bore the sin of many, and made intercession for the transgressors* (Isaiah 53:1-12).

The part of the verse that says, "By his wounds we are healed" is the prophecy made before Messiah had come; it speaks of something that is in process. The apostle Peter would update this promised word when he wrote,

> *He himself bore our sins" in his body on the cross, so that we might die to sins and live for righteousness; "by his wounds **you have been healed**"* (1 Peter 2:24).

Peter wrote about our healing in the present perfect progressive tense, which describes an action that started in the past, continues in the present, and may continue into the future. In other words, Jesus has completely covered the cost of all our healing in advance; it is now yours to access.

Jesus Christ your loving Savior paid the price for your healing over two thousand years ago. Your faith is the check that has the full backing of the Bank of Heaven to cover your health costs in full. Furthermore, Jesus has given you the authority to sign it in His name with His full endorsement.

That is why we serve an awesome God; His salvation has covered us with everything we need for this life and our future home in heaven.

Prayer

Lord, You are so good to me, and I thank You for all You have done for me. Because of that, I do not want to insult You by ignoring the gifts You have given to me. Thank You for giving us the gift of healing, and I ask for its release in my body this day. Let me live all of my days in Your divine health. In Jesus' name, I pray.

Declaration

Because of You, my wonderful Lord and Savior, I believe and receive my total healing. Every health issue known or unknown, I bring it by faith to the place where Jesus bore it in His own body for my healing. I call to remembrance all that Jesus has accomplished and declare that my body must conform to the victory Jesus has won for me. Divine health resides in every cell of my body. In Jesus' name, I declare it done. Amen.

> *My son, pay attention to my words; incline your ear to my sayings.*

*Do not lose sight of them; keep them within your heart.
For they are life to those who find them, and health to the whole body* (Proverbs 4:20-22).

Day 13

Lazarus - Part 1

This is the first of a three-part devotional on the raising of Lazarus from the dead.
In those times when you feel all is lost and your faith is gone, it is never over when Jesus is present.

Lazarus' Story

At this time a man named Lazarus was sick. He lived in Bethany, the village of Mary and her sister Martha. (Mary, whose brother Lazarus was sick, would later anoint the Lord with perfume and wipe His feet with her hair.) So the sisters sent word to Jesus, "Lord, the one You love is sick."
When Jesus heard this, He said, "This sickness will not end in death. No, it is for the glory of God, so that the Son of God may be glorified through it."
Now Jesus loved Martha and her sister and Lazarus. So on hearing that Lazarus was sick, He stayed where He was for two days, and then

He said to the disciples, "Let us go back to Judea."
"Rabbi," they replied, "the Jews just tried to stone You, and You are going back there?" Jesus answered, "Are there not twelve hours of daylight? If anyone walks in the daytime, he will not stumble, because he sees by the light of this world. But if anyone walks at night, he will stumble, because he has no light."
After He had said this, He told them, "Our friend Lazarus has fallen asleep, but I am going there to wake him up."
His disciples replied, "Lord, if he is sleeping, he will get better." They thought that Jesus was talking about actual sleep, but He was speaking about the death of Lazarus.
So Jesus told them plainly, "Lazarus is dead, and for your sake I am glad I was not there, so that you may believe. But let us go to him."
Then Thomas called Didymus said to his fellow disciples, "Let us also go, so that we may die with Him." When Jesus arrived, He found that Lazarus had already spent four days in the tomb (John 11:1-17)

When you face a health crisis, the distressing rippling effect makes its way through to your family and friends. I can think of no chapter in the New Testament that gives us a more compelling and in-depth look at what takes place when tragedy strikes a family as what we will read in John Chapter 11.

Jesus had a great friendship with Mary, Martha, and Lazarus. He loved this family and visited with them whenever He had a chance. They lived in Bethany, in the province of Judea, which was about a mile and a half from Jerusalem. That area was now hostile territory for Jesus, for the religious leadership in Jerusalem was seeking to arrest Him and have Him killed. Galilee is where Jesus mostly resided and was a safe place for Him and His disciples to operate without the danger of arrest. But tragedy struck this family. Mary and Martha sent word to Jesus concerning the worsening condition of their brother. When Jesus received the news from the messenger, He said aloud for all to hear,

> *This sickness will not end in death. No, it is for the glory of God, so that the Son of God may be glorified through it* (John 11:4).

That was the message Jesus sent back to the family and those who brought the news. With that word, they took comfort and set out to make the long journey home. This must have been the most reassuring word that they could have hoped to hear. Certainly, that news and the fact that Jesus was on the way would have buoyed their faith. I am sure that Lazarus thought once the Lord arrived, his health crisis would be a thing of the past. He had witnessed and seen the numerous healings and deliverances that took place at the mere touch of Jesus or from a word spoken by Him. But hour-by-hour, Lazarus' condition worsened and everyone's anxiety level kept rising.

Jesus had sent His word figuratively and spiritually, which stated that Lazarus' sickness would not end in death. Time was lapsing and Lazarus was beginning to fade. As the hours passed so too would Lazarus. After two days, Jesus told the disciples to their shock, that they would be heading to Bethany. They pleaded with Him not to go because it was a close call the last time they were in Jerusalem; the crowds threatened to stone the Lord. The disciples heard from Jesus' own words that Lazarus would not die, so they could not figure out why in the world Jesus wanted to risk His safety and theirs by going back in the vicinity of Jerusalem.

They didn't understand that Jesus was speaking words of faith about Lazarus' sleeping and recovery. In the book of Romans, Paul wrote,

> *The God who gives life to the dead and calls into being what does not yet exist* (Romans 4:17b).

Jesus was already calling into being the things that were not as though they concerned Lazarus. He was speaking faith-filled words by saying that Lazarus was sleeping. However, He had to speak in plain language concerning his death because the disciples just did not understand what He was doing.

If Mary, Martha, and Lazarus had received Jesus' initial words as an authoritative decree in the way the centurion soldier perceived it, then Jesus could have been spared the trip. Somehow, they had come to the conclusion that Jesus had to personally come and pray over their brother. The word of healing had already been sent and present in their situation; they just needed to lay hold of it by faith.

At this point, the story makes its way to us. You don't need an appearance from Jesus. You don't need those from a great healing ministry to come and pray for you. You don't need a prayer vigil to be started for you. All you need is a word from Jesus, and you have that from His words given to us in the New Testament. They are a living will and testament from Him to every generation. All we have to do is simply believe and take Him at His word. Doing so honors and pleases Him more than any other request we could make. Take ownership of these healing scriptures, and let them accomplish their work, for they are part of your inheritance in Christ.

We will continue this story in tomorrow's devotion.

Prayer

Lord, let these testimonies of Your love and power spring forth in my life and grow to be an immovable tree of faith in my life. Show me any hindrances to my belief and trust in You and Your Word. I pray this in Jesus' name. Amen.

Declaration

I declare that the Word of God is as true and real for me as it was true and real for them. Therefore, I take You at Your word. I take Your Word and apply it to my situation. I am healed. I am blessed. I am prospering and in good health. This is my statement of faith for all the days of my life. In Jesus' name.

> *He sent his word, and healed them, and delivered them from their destructions (Psalm 107:20).*

Day 14

Lazarus - Part 2

We continue this look into John Chapter 11 from the perspective of Martha and her desperate dialogue with Jesus over her brother.

Martha's Story

> *Now Bethany was near Jerusalem, a little less than two miles away, and many of the Jews had come to Martha and Mary to console them in the loss of their brother. So when Martha heard that Jesus was coming, she went out to meet Him; but Mary stayed at home.*
> *Martha said to Jesus, "Lord, if You had been here, my brother would not have died. But even now I know that God will give You whatever You ask Him."*
> *"Your brother will rise again," Jesus told her.*
> *Martha replied, "I know that he will rise again in the resurrection at the last day."*
> *Jesus said to her, "I am the resurrection and the life. He who*

> *believes in Me will live, even though he dies. And everyone who lives and believes in Me will never die. Do you believe this?" "Yes, Lord," she answered, "I believe that You are the Christ, the Son of God, who was to come into the world."*
> *After Martha had said this, she went back and called her sister Mary aside to tell her, "The Teacher is here and is asking for you." And when Mary heard this, she got up quickly and went to Him* (John 11:18-29).

As we move further into the story of Lazarus, we read of how Martha handled her brother's death. Jesus had sent them word that her brother would live but now she was sitting there staring at his corpse. How could this be? How could Jesus be so wrong? When she heard that Jesus had finally arrived in town, she didn't hesitate. Immediately, she went out to meet Him.

She was a conflicted soul. This is evident in the first words she said to the Lord. She blamed Him for her brother's death because He did not come to their aid quickly enough. The second thing she uttered came from her belief in Him as the Messiah. Martha equated her brother's healing with the Lord's physical presence. Jesus equated that

His manifest power is revealed through believing in who He is and what He says. The issue is not whether you see or feel His presence; the issue is do you believe He is who He says He is?

Like a fisherman, Jesus cast a line of faith to Martha, but she didn't fully take it. Instead, she responded with the hope of a future afterlife. That is how believers respond when their faith is not activated. They have the anchor of the hope of heaven, which in and of itself is a good thing, but it won't bring the power of God into the present. Hope is the promise of a tomorrow, while faith is a "now" reality for today. Hope is static, biding its time for a future day, while faith is active and on the move, reaching into the promises of God for the present. When the crisis of life hits, you have to weigh anchor, raise your sails of faith and move into your desired result through your belief and trust in Jesus. That is what Jesus was trying to do for Martha. He was speaking words of life to move her into a believing trust in Him.

Martha's response to Jesus deferred His glory to a future time, but Jesus pressed the issue to the present time. A belief centered on a future hope will not bring the power of God into the present. What you are believing for must be in the "here and now" because it is through a "now" faith that the resources of the kingdom of God are engaged and released. Jesus was emphatically saying that He is the source of all life, and He rules over death. The resurrection is not a future event; the resurrection is a person, and that person is Jesus. The Lord has the final say on all matters of life and death. Jesus was going after how Martha believed to get her belief aligned with the Lord so that her faith could become effectual.

With great sensitivity to how fragile Martha was at that time, He continued to speak words of faith and life to her. The Lord was asking her to believe in something that was unheard of in Israel or anywhere for that matter. How could a person who has been dead for four days be brought back to life? The Jews of the first century buried their dead within 24 hours, and they believed that the person's spirit would hover over its body for three days. I suppose that since it had become the fourth day, the finality of death was now a symbolic certainty.

Slowly but surely, Martha started to grasp that Jesus was the final authority over death. She came to the realization that the Lord was about to do something miraculous. It was then that Martha went to get her sister to meet with Jesus. The Lord dearly loved this family, so it would be a reasonable question to ask, "Why did He allow them to go through this painful heartbreak?" Why couldn't He just pray and speak a word to raise Lazarus as we have read about in the other devotions on healing? There is only one identifiable difference between this and the other accounts that we read about in the biblical testimonies of healing. Their faith had not been engaged with the Lord, and this was a critical component to keep the family members connected to the miracle.

There is something else to consider, which could be part of the broader picture for all concerned. I am sure this would not have been an easy decision for the Lord to make for His friends, but it was also equally important. The Lord knew that He only had a few more days on the earth. Hence, what would take place for Lazarus and this family would establish a foundation for their lives and walk of faith forever. Oftentimes, our greatest trials by fire shape and prepare us for our destiny in God. What you endure and subsequently overcome by faith and trust in Him will often be the bedrock and the basis to build something great in your life.

Martha and Mary needed something vitally important to be established in them through this crisis. If Jesus had just acted immediately and used His faith to meet their need, in their next time of crisis, they would be in the same boat looking for Jesus, and He would not be physically there. But, if the Lord could teach them that they can completely rely on His Word even in His absence, they would still see His power manifest. What we see through their difficult learning experience is what we all need to take hold of and believe in our lives.

Jesus is the resurrection and the life. He is a faithful God in whom we can trust. Just as He gave Martha and Mary His word concerning Lazarus, we have been given His Word through the scriptures. His Word addresses all of our needs; it is alive and powerful through the Holy Spirit. The Holy Spirit is our Comforter in every situation we face. He instructs us what we need to do to see His power released. He counsels and coaches us in the same way Jesus talked Martha through to a victorious conclusion for her family.

Meditate on God's words and promises. Listen for that still, small voice in your heart speaking words of faith and life to you. Know that even a voice that shouts as loud as death cannot prevail over the gentlest whisper coming from the one who is life. No word coming from a man is greater than God's Word coming to you by His Spirit. When we know this in the core of our beings, it makes us fearless in this life.

In tomorrow's devotion, we will complete the story of this family's miracle.

Prayer

Lord, help me to be as one who is not swayed by any negative report or thought, no matter how serious it may be. Give me a hunger and a passion for Your Word, for I know that faith comes and grows by hearing Your words in the scriptures. Help me to be ever aware of the presence of the Holy Spirit and to always keep a listening ear to His subtle promptings and His instructions. In doing these things, I know that they will keep my eyes on You and keep my trust focused on You for a sure victory in whatever I will face. In Jesus' name, I pray.

Declaration

Lord, You are the resurrection and the life, and nothing you proclaim to be alive can remain dead. Therefore, I speak life to my every situation and declare that which appears to be dead must come alive. I speak life into every situation that is gasping for breath, and I declare full recovery, as well as health to my every need by the power and mighty name of Jesus. I praise You and thank You for Your grace and power that is already at work in me.

*Consider it pure joy, my brothers, when you encounter trials of many kinds, because you know that the testing of your faith develops perseverance. Allow perseverance to finish its work, so that you may be mature and complete, not lacking anything.
If any of you lacks wisdom, he should ask God, who gives generously to all without finding fault, and it will be given to him. But he must ask in faith, without doubting, because he who doubts is like a wave of the sea, blown and tossed by the wind. That man should not expect to receive anything from the Lord. He is a double-minded man, unstable in all his ways* (James 1:2-8).

Day 15

Lazarus - Part 3

This is the final segment from John Chapter 11, which brings our focus on the dialogue between Jesus and Mary prior to the raising of Lazarus.

Mary's Story and Lazarus' Four-day Tour of the Afterlife Ends

> *Now Jesus had not yet entered the village, but was still at the place where Martha had met Him. When the Jews who were in the house consoling Mary saw how quickly she got up and went out, they followed her, supposing she was going to the tomb to mourn there. When Mary came to Jesus and saw Him, she fell at His feet and said, "Lord, if You had been here, my brother would not have died."*
> *When Jesus saw her weeping, and the Jews who had come with her also weeping, He was deeply moved in spirit and troubled. "Where have you laid him?" He asked.*
> *"Come and see, Lord," they answered.*

Jesus wept.
Then the Jews said, "See how He loved him!"
But some of them asked, "Could not this man who opened the eyes of the blind also have kept Lazarus from dying?"
Jesus, once again deeply moved, came to the tomb. It was a cave with a stone laid across the entrance.
"Take away the stone," Jesus said.
"Lord, by now he stinks," said Martha, the sister of the dead man. "It has already been four days."
Jesus replied, "Did I not tell you that if you believed, you would see the glory of God?"
So they took away the stone. Then Jesus lifted His eyes upward and said, "Father, I thank You that You have heard Me. I knew that You always hear Me, but I say this for the benefit of the people standing here, so they may believe that You sent Me."
After Jesus had said this, He called out in a loud voice, "Lazarus, come out!"
The man who had been dead came out with his hands and feet bound in strips of linen, and his face wrapped in a headcloth. "Unwrap him and let

him go," Jesus told them (John 11:30-44)

When Mary heard that Jesus had finally arrived in town, she just sat there numb and confused over what had happened. In the past, whenever Jesus was with them, she would give Him her complete attention and devotion. She would hang onto every word that He said. It didn't matter that it would get her in trouble with Martha who would be left to do all the serving; nothing was going to deprive her of one second of time with her beloved Messiah and friend. But now, the one she so loved and trusted had seemingly failed her family and let them down.

It is clear that Mary and Martha came to the same conclusion concerning their brother's death. They inadvertently blamed Jesus believing His lack of urgency in coming in their critical time of need was the reason for Lazarus' passing. Like Mary and Martha, sometimes we think that just because we do not see Jesus or get an immediate response from Him that He has somehow let us down. But God does see and hear, and in their case, He had already presided over the matter some four days earlier by stating that this sickness was not unto death. In fact, He had promised that it would bring glory to God.

As we have read through this passage, you can see everyone's emotions were raw and on the surface. They loved Jesus, and He loved this family. It is from this passage that we read the shortest verse in the Bible, which is "Jesus wept." But there is something that the Greek language reveals in this passage that is not easily communicated in English. "He was deeply moved in spirit and troubled" (John 11:33) is translated from the Greek word, *enebrimēsato*, which carries within its meaning an anger or a snort of contempt over the entire situation. Jesus was not going to allow His friends to suffer a moment longer. He was in battle mode and was intent on reclaiming that man's life.

It's at this point that the friends of the family arrived and everyone was talking about what had happened. They were also questioning why Jesus couldn't or didn't help this family. When Jesus commanded that the tomb be opened, Martha shifted again to unbelief by telling Jesus that the corpse was decomposing. Jesus had to coach her back into belief and walked her back through the things He told her earlier. Her natural senses had once again taken hold of her over her spiritual sense. This is understandable and, yet again, Jesus had to bring that focus back to who He is and His mighty power, not on what she saw. Jesus reminded Martha that if she believes, she would see the power of God. There is something so important about family members staying in faith for their loved ones in a time of crisis. We see throughout these testimonies of healing that the Lord kept encouraging those loved ones to believe on behalf of their family members. It is especially true in a situation when the person can no longer intercede for himself; someone has to rise up and be that intercessor for that loved one.

The Lord empathized with Martha and Mary knowing the emotional strain they were under. But in order to keep their hope alive, He had to continue drawing their focus back to Him. It is like being a diver whose tank has gone to empty and you are gasping for air. Jesus is diving with you in that situation, and every time you look to Him, He gives you air to breathe from His tank. His tank is never empty, and He will keep giving you air until you can rise up safely and get back to the surface. Stepping out in faith is not a fragile thing like a house of cards that will fall at the first thought of doubt. It is more like building a bridge in good weather or bad; the work continues. You keep persevering to its completion in order to get to the other side. That other side is where the miracle is because that ground is the kingdom of God. The Lord is there with you helping you through all the ups and downs of your believing, so you can successfully finish that bridge of faith.

Jesus pushed through all of the unbelief, commanded Lazarus to come forth and out he came. Death had to surrender Lazarus to Jesus. In like manner, every challenge you face will also be forced to surrender to the name of Jesus on your lips. Keep your heart focused on the lovingkindness of God and not on the circumstances, even when you feel you can't see or hear Him. Remember this fact: it may not be a word that was given a few days ago as in the case of Martha and Mary, but it is a word that was given to you two thousand years ago. God's Word is eternal. Jesus presided over your situation and gave you His Word and promise through His cross. All of God's promises are as true now as they were then, we are told to simply believe.

Rise up in faith, and your Lazarus situation will do the same.

Prayer

Heavenly Father, raise to life all of the hopes I once held that now seem to have died. You are the resurrection and the life; fill my lungs with Your spiritual oxygen that I can breathe again. Let each breath of faith bring life to the promises that You have given through Your Word. Thank You,

Lord, for Your goodness and mercy. In Jesus' name. Amen.

Declaration

In Jesus' name, I speak into my need the way Jesus spoke to Lazarus, and I call you to arise from the dead. I infuse everything that appears to be negative with words of faith and life that are anointed by the Lord. I am healed. I am well. I am prospering in all of the graces that are freely given by God. I declare that I too will have a testimony of life, not death.

> *All the nations you have made will come and worship before you, Lord; they will bring glory to your name. For you are great and do marvelous deeds; you alone are God.*
> *Teach me your way, LORD, that I may rely on your faithfulness; give me an undivided heart, that I may fear your name.*
> *I will praise you, Lord my God, with all my heart; I will glorify your name forever.*
> *For great is your love toward me; you have delivered me from the depths, from the realm of the dead* (Psalm 86:9-13).

Day 16

After Eighteen Years, Her Sabbath Rest Had Come

When religious dogmas seek to override the mercy of God, they become His adversaries. This woman's story is the reason Jesus and religion have very little in common.

The Healing and Deliverance of the Woman with a Crippling Back Injury

One Sabbath Jesus was teaching in one of the synagogues, and a woman there had been disabled by a spirit for eighteen years. She was hunched over and could not stand up straight. When Jesus saw her, He called her over and said, "Woman, you are set free from your infirmity." Then He laid His hands on her, and immediately she straightened up and began to glorify God.
But the synagogue leader was indignant that Jesus had healed on the Sabbath. "There are six days for work," he told the crowd. "So come and be healed on those days and not on the Sabbath."

> *"You hypocrites!" the Lord replied, "Does not each of you on the Sabbath untie his ox or donkey from the stall and lead it to water? Then should not this daughter of Abraham, whom Satan has bound for eighteen long years, be released from her bondage on the Sabbath day?"*
> *When Jesus said this, all His adversaries were humiliated. And the whole crowd rejoiced at all the glorious things He was doing* (Luke 13:10-17).

In this account, we read of a woman with a disabling condition that left her hunched over for eighteen years. The confrontation that ensued over her healing reflected an ongoing battle between Jesus and the religious authorities. Throughout the Gospels, the heart of Jesus is being expressed to the lost, the downcast, and those who are suffering. He offers hope, compassion, and kindness to those people. On the other hand, when you see Jesus dealing with the religious authorities of His day, He offers them only disdain and rebuke.

These were the so-called shepherds of Israel to whom the Lord had committed the care of His flock. Sadly, they had become so hardened in their self-righteousness, that the observances of religious rules were deemed to be more important than a person in need. They had violated the very nature of God by their loveless ministry, which left them nothing to offer their people except a cold, hard religion.

The leader of the synagogue had become one of the shepherds Jesus warned about in John Chapter 10. A wonderful miracle took place for someone in his congregation. However, instead of having joy over the healing, he took offense and rebuked the Lord. This woman had been delivered from a spirit of infirmity that caused her to suffer for eighteen years; yet, it was deemed as nothing to that man because all he saw was a violation of the rules. If Jesus had obeyed their interpretation of what the Sabbath was for, that woman would have remained in her condition. Who would know if she and Jesus would have ever crossed paths again? The Lord was not going to let that scenario happen or cater to their loveless interpretation of the Law of Moses.

I am going to say something that may surprise or shock you. The Lord has little regard for your religious beliefs or those of your spiritual leaders if those beliefs are blind to His desire to show mercy and compassion. Your church, denomination or religion is essentially useless to Him if it is not for the well-being and service of others. Religious thinking will serve its own end and justify its actions while neglecting the needs of those it should be serving. That is what Jesus was implying when He said to them that they would untie their oxen and take them to water, which was a violation of the Sabbath. Here is Jesus untying a woman from the bondage of a disabling spirit. Yet, they cry foul and seethe with contempt against Jesus for breaking their rules. They had no consideration for the person in need. A religious belief that exalts a judge's gavel to render judgment instead of offering mercy is religion gone wrong. When religious dogma supersedes mercy, it is due to a failure in understanding the good news that Jesus Christ brought to the world.

> *For God loved the world so much that he gave his one and only Son, so that everyone who believes in him will not perish but have eternal life. For God did not send His Son into the world to condemn the world, but to save the world through Him* (John 3:16, 17).

Jesus came to save the world. It should please us all to know that the Greek word *sozo*, which is translated as "save," offers within its meaning healing as one of the benefits of the Lord's offered salvation. You cannot earn salvation; it is a free gift from God and comes through your belief that Jesus is the Christ of God. That simple recognition of the truth places you on a fast track to receiving your healing. That woman who had suffered so severely would soon understand this about Jesus.

When God appointed the Sabbath, it was meant as a gift of rest and freedom from the toil of labor. For eighteen years, this woman did not have a single day of rest from her suffering and pain. When Jesus saw her, He was determined not to let it continue a day longer and delivered her from her condition. One can only imagine what it meant to that dear woman to be able to walk upright and be pain- free after all those years. The relief and the joy she felt must have been overwhelming to her and all those who truly cared for her. She too could now experience what rest was like on the Sabbath, for Jesus who is the Sabbath rest for mankind had entered her life.

Nothing within the story indicates that this woman's faith was activated or that she was ready to receive her healing. However, what you do see through this testimony of healing is that the Lord had seen her in her condition. He was determined to help her and set her free from that demonic oppression. He knew it would incite the religious leaders against Him, but He cared for her more than He cared for His own well-being. Do you think God cares any less for you in your situation?

It is not mere happenstance that these messages are found in the Bible. They were placed there to show us that what was true for the people described in the scriptures is also true for us. Jesus is your rest from any condition you are suffering from and toiling under. He holds no gavel in His hand. His heart is not hardened to the cry of your heart. He loves you dearly and knew you before you were born. Any infirmity or sickness is not your lot in life nor is it His will. Jesus bore suffering in His own body that you could be free from the suffering in your body. Believe this to be true for you and the circumstances of your life will have to bow and yield to this truth.

Prayer

Heavenly Father, awaken my heart to rise up and believe it is Your good pleasure to give us all the benefits of Your kingdom. Help me to see that You are greater than any challenge I face and that Your love for me resounds with a big yes in response to my request to be healed. Thank You in advance for the healing released into my body. In Jesus' name, I pray.

Declaration

I believe what I have just read is true for me and that I am beloved in Your eyes. I believe Your heart overflows with love for me and that You care for my well-being. Therefore, I believe that healing is my right and recovery must take place in my body. Jesus is my Sabbath right and rest for my body from all affliction and pain. I declare that this truth is my reality. In Jesus' name!

> *Surely he took up our pain and bore our suffering, yet we considered him punished by God, stricken by him, and afflicted.*
> *But he was pierced for our transgressions, he was crushed for our iniquities; the punishment that brought us peace was on him, and by his wounds we are healed. We all, like sheep, have gone astray, each of us has turned to our own way; and the Lord has laid on him the iniquity of us all* (Isaiah 53:4-6).

Day 17

A Withered Hand Is Healed

Here again, Jesus faces another confrontation over healing that takes place on the Sabbath.

The War against the Spirit of Religion Continues

> *On another Sabbath, Jesus entered the synagogue and was teaching, and a man was there whose right hand was withered. Looking for a reason to accuse Jesus, the scribes and Pharisees were watching Him closely to see if He would heal on the Sabbath.*
> *But Jesus knew their thoughts and said to the man with the withered hand, "Get up and stand among us." So he got up and stood there. Then Jesus said to them, "I ask you, which is lawful on the Sabbath: to do good or to do evil, to save life or to destroy it?" And after looking around at all of them, He said to the man, "Stretch out your hand." He did so, and it was restored.*

But the scribes and Pharisees were filled with rage and began to discuss with one another what they might do to Jesus (Luke 6:6-11).

On another Sabbath, Jesus was in attendance at a synagogue in the town where He was ministering. In what was becoming a common occurrence, He found Himself in conflict with the religious establishment. Once again, it was over issues concerning what was allowed on the Sabbath.

It's a sad day when the spirit of religion can so blind a person's heart that he only perceives the religious offense and cannot see the love of God in action. What was designed to be a gift of rest for the people of God had now become legalistic labor. A day to commune with God and family would become a day of trying to obey rules that religion imposed. These rules seemed endless as to what you could or couldn't do. There were rules on how far you could travel, how you prepared your food, even how many strokes a woman could do while brushing her hair, and on and on it went. What was meant to be a blessing of rest became a burden and toil.

When Jesus said that the Sabbath was made for man, He was revealing the Father's true heart on the matter, for it was to be a day of blessing for His people. In fact, all of the commandments hold the DNA of God's love within them. That is why Jesus issued only one commandment and that was to love one another. That truth was always there hidden in the Ten Commandments, for if you are truly walking in love toward another person, you really can't break any of them. But, when you subtract a relationship with God from the equation, all you are left with are rules of conduct that will eventually be your judge.

In returning to the story, a man was in the congregation with some form of deformity in his hand. There was no healthcare or social assistance; if you couldn't work, your only option was to beg. The fact that he had a withered hand would probably mean that it was very difficult to earn an income. Every day of his life would have been a challenge and toil. Where was his freedom from labor? Where was his Sabbath rest?

Every circumcision that took place on the Sabbath was a technical violation of the day of rest. So, the removal of a part of the body was acceptable to the religious mind, but the restoration of a part of the body was not. That is the essence of religious hypocrisy.

Jesus saw the man and called him to stand front and center before the entire congregation. Once again, the Lord would try to penetrate the hardened hearts of those religious leaders in attendance. Can you imagine the scene that took place when Jesus healed that man's hand? All those in attendance saw that wonderful, creative miracle taking place before their eyes. Probably, most of them knew the man and the celebration of his healing must have blown the roof off that place. It should have brought great joy to the leaders of that synagogue because one of their own people had experienced such marvelous healing? It should have, but it didn't. Instead, they were filled with rage and wanted to get rid of Jesus in the worst possible way. This act of healing emboldened the religious establishment even more to plot the Lord's death. As for the man with the restored hand, he learned the real meaning of the Sabbath rest and received a life without handicap. He was freed from the daily challenge of trying to do with one hand what others could do with two.

So what are we to glean from a story such as this? What can we apply to our lives? My response to that question begins with another question: what religious arguments, wrong teachings, and beliefs are stumbling blocks in your mind preventing your healing from God? Do you feel something you did in your past disqualifies you? Is it a teaching or a belief you were taught by someone you respect that always comes to your mind and casts doubts upon your faith to be healed?

We are all in the same fight with the spirit of religion Jesus battled. These battlegrounds are in our thoughts and they try to drag us down to hopelessness and unbelief. Paul the apostle described how to deal with these attacks to our faith by writing,

> *For though we live in the flesh, we do not wage war according to the flesh. The weapons of our warfare are not the weapons of the world. Instead, they have divine power to demolish strongholds. We tear down arguments, and every presumption set up against the knowledge of God; and we take captive every thought to make it obedient to Christ* (2 Corinthians 10:3-5).

Treat any thought that casts doubts on your healing as an enemy, and cast it down. Any thought that tells you God is against you being healed is against the knowledge of God and needs to be taken captive. To take it captive is to shut it up in a prison, which will then shut up its voice in your heart. That will win the battle and lead you one step closer to winning the war.

Prayer

Lord, give me wisdom and discernment to separate truth from the beliefs that I have embraced in my life concerning Your will and my healing. Help me to recognize the heart of Jesus in every situation I face and esteem His words as my final authority on any given matter. Give me a greater understanding of Your love for me that would keep me afloat through any troubled waters that are before me. In Jesus' name, I trust You and make this request.

Declaration

In the name of Jesus, I cast down every thought, every held belief and any unbelief that would seek to deny my healing from the Lord. I call unbelief an enemy, and I take those thoughts of doubt captive. I declare my body is a sickness free zone and say that divine health is mine. I claim this as my right in Christ. Amen.

> *Come to Me, all you who are weary and burdened, and I will give you rest. Take My yoke upon you and learn from Me; for I am gentle and humble in heart, and you will find rest for your souls. For My yoke is easy and My burden is light* (Matthew 11:28-30).

Day 18

Jesus Elevates a Person's Value

Once again, Jesus was at war against hardened religious doctrine. He was relentless in His desire to reclaim the Sabbath for mankind and restore true rest to His people.

Jesus Heals a Man with Dropsy

> *One Sabbath, Jesus went to eat in the home of a leading Pharisee, and those in attendance were watching Him closely. Right there in front of Him was a man with dropsy. So Jesus asked the experts in the law and the Pharisees, "Is it lawful to heal on the Sabbath or not?"*
> *But they remained silent.*
> *Then Jesus took hold of the man, healed him, and sent him on his way. And He asked them, "Which of you whose son or ox falls into a pit on the Sabbath day will not immediately pull him out?" And they were unable to answer these questions* (Luke 14:1-5).

As you read these testimonies of healing in the New Testament, you are surely noticing a continuing pattern. The Sabbath day had become a constant source of conflict between Jesus and the religious establishment. Picture what it would be like if Jesus had shown up at your church and the leadership became angry and offended because He was not abiding by their traditions and rules. That may seem to be ridiculous on the surface, but the sad reality is that I don't think the reaction Jesus faced then would be any different today. How many churches would truly welcome Jesus? Or would they just consider Him a disruptive element to their status quo?

It would be easy to make the assumption that Jesus was trying to pick a spiritual fight against the religious order of the day. But in reality, the primary purpose of Jesus was to seek the lost and hurting of His nation and restore them spiritually and physically. He saw the nation as sheep without a true shepherd. The shepherds who were over the sheep were mistreating them and would abandon them whenever a potential threat arose.

Jesus went to the synagogue because it was there that the people gathered as a community before the Lord. It was there that Jesus saw the needs of the people. He loved them too much to sit idly by and let another day pass while they suffered from their afflictions.

The Lord's conflicts with religious leaders had become commonplace throughout His ministry. He appealed to their compassion and human decency but would only be met with cold, harsh, and rigid responses to upholding their traditions and rules. People who were created in the image of God were taught that religious acceptance was only possible if they offered servitude to its rules. The God who they claimed to worship was standing before them, but they could not recognize Him. Similarly, Jesus could not even recognize the religion that was founded to worship God, who He was. The religious leaders had created a massive ritual of rules that no longer required God's participation or His presence.

And here, in the midst of all this, stood a man who was suffering from dropsy.

Love Triumphs over Religion

Dropsy in the modern vernacular is the condition called edema. It is characterized by an excess of watery fluid in the cavities or tissues of the body and is due to congestive heart failure. Another form of edema is a condition called pulmonary edema, which is when fluid collects in the air sacs of your lungs. It affects a person's breathing causing a feeling of suffocation or as if drowning due to fluid building up in the lungs. Maybe the Lord used the analogy of a person or animal falling into a well to similarly portray one who is in danger of drowning. The Greek word *phrear* translates into English as a pit or a well and is used in this passage of scripture. Regardless of what form of dropsy it was, the man was suffering and needed a miracle.

What has happened to the Lord's shepherds that they are so indifferent to the well-being of His sheep? Jesus asked them a simple question, and you could have heard a pin drop as nobody said a word in response. It was then that Jesus took hold of the man, probably with a hug that carried the weight of God Almighty's compassion and healed him on the spot. Jesus then asked a rhetorical question that should have brought an obvious answer: "Which of you whose son or ox falls into a pit on the Sabbath day will not immediately pull him out?" (Luke 14:5). He knew that all of them would have led the rescue, even though it meant they would have violated the ritual-laden Sabbath. How did it get to the point that an animal could have more value to these religious leaders than a person who is suffering?

This was not the first time the Lord used this analogy when dealing with the religious leaders. However, His words were not breaking through their hardened hearts. You will not read of Jesus being in conflict with people no matter what their sins were, but you will always read of His conflicts with a cold, self-righteous religious establishment.

This constant violation by Jesus of healing people on the Sabbath became one of the greatest reasons for their seething hatred of Him. It would cause them to reject Him as a prophet and Messiah and lead to the plotting of His death. None of this mattered to Jesus because His love for those who were suffering was greater than His care for His own life.

Your well-being means as much to the Lord as any of those people whose accounts of healings are recorded in Scripture. Just as He would look around in the synagogue and identify the hurting and afflicted, He looks for yours. Your situation has also not escaped His sight. No matter what you are contending with in your life, know this: God loves you, and He has a Sabbath rest waiting for you. He wants you well and whole with a life full of days because every day is a Sabbath rest in Christ. If you harbor any belief in your heart or mind that is contrary to what I have just written, get rid of it and cast those thoughts down. Whatever thinking or belief pit you have fallen into, know this: Jesus is reaching into it to pull you out of it. Treat those thoughts with the same resistance Jesus had against a hardened, religious spirit and then believe that the Lord has singled you out for healing. He is ready, willing and able to pull you out of that pit of sickness and hopelessness and is calling you forward, for your time has come.

Prayer

Lord, just as You did for the man in this story, call me forward to demonstrate Your healing mercy to family, friends, and my community. Awaken belief in me to know the love and healing that is found in Your embrace. In Jesus' name, I pray. Amen.

Declaration

I am precious in the sight of God and favored. I stand before You in Your embrace and declare myself blessed, whole, and enveloped in divine health. Faith works by love and I believe in Your love for me. Sickness and disease must go in Jesus' name. I declare that I will dwell in health for all of my days.

> *Beloved, I pray that in every way you may prosper and*

enjoy good health, as your soul also prospers (3 John 1:2).

Day 19

The DNA of Jesus

The next series of devotions will look at the unconventional ways that Jesus healed people during His ministry on the earth.

A Deaf Person Hears and His Speech Is Loosed

> *Then Jesus left the region of Tyre and went through Sidon to the Sea of Galilee and into the region of the Decapolis. Some people brought to Him a man who was deaf and hardly able to speak, and they begged Jesus to place His hand on him.*
> *So Jesus took him aside privately, away from the crowd, and put His fingers into the man's ears. Then He spit and touched the man's tongue. And looking up to heaven, He sighed deeply and said to him, "Ephphatha!" (which means, "Be opened!"). Immediately the man's ears were opened and his tongue was released, and he began to speak plainly. Jesus ordered them not to tell anyone. But the more He ordered them, the more widely they*

> *proclaimed it. The people were utterly astonished and said, "He has done all things well! He makes even the deaf to hear and the mute to speak!"* (Mark 7:31-37).

What is so interesting about this story is how Jesus handled the healing of this man who was deaf and mute. His friends or family had brought him to Jesus and their faith believed that Jesus' touch would heal him. That is the picture of intercession when we bring others before the Lord and petition God on their behalf. His family and friends were acting on their faith by their actions, just as a person who brings someone before the Lord spiritually through prayer.

Jesus took the man aside privately to minister to him. Why did he do that? Clearly, the people who brought him to Jesus had demonstrated their faith by their actions, so what was the reason for the Lord's decision?

Jesus removed everyone from seeing how He would minister to this man because what He would do next might have changed their faith. The Lord was keeping their faith connected to this man, and He would partner with them for the man's healing. Remember, faith is initiated through hearing God's Word. The Gospel of John declares that

Jesus is the Word of God made flesh who lived among those of John's day. The hearing of God's Word to instill faith was irrelevant to this man because he couldn't hear. Therefore, the faith of others would be very important for the man to receive his healing.

I don't think anyone would have taken notice of Jesus putting his fingers into the man's ears when He prayed. However, when Jesus spat on His hand and then put it into the man's mouth, it may well have undone the faith of those who brought the man. I'm sure the Lord's actions could have caused many to be offended by Him if they saw what He did. That is precisely why Jesus took the man aside. What is equally surprising is the man saw what Jesus was doing and let Him do it. The man had enough faith to allow Jesus to pray for him in this most unusual way and the results of his healing were immediate. From this story, we see a collective faith coming from everyone involved and the Lord's use of His DNA.

The DNA of Jesus is the essence of the living God, and that is what this testimony is about. DNA is an acronym for deoxyribonucleic acid. It is the molecule that contains the genetic code of who you are and where you came from. If you ever took a DNA test to find out more about your ancestry, you would have submitted a sample of your spittle, which contains your DNA.

Jesus touched the man's tongue with His fingers that He spat upon; by doing so, He placed a part of His life into that man. Every cell of the physical body of Jesus was infused with the power and life of the almighty God, and He had just given that man a small sample. That small sample was more than enough to open the man's ears, loose his tongue, and restore his speech.

It may surprise you to know that when you believed on Jesus and were born again, His DNA was infused in your spirit. Thus, you carry within you the nature of God. The Holy Spirit resides in you, and you too can do the works of Jesus. The Lord even promised that His people would do greater works than He did on the earth because He would be with His Father.

> *Truly, truly, I tell you, whoever believes in Me will also do the works that I am doing. He will do even greater things than these, because I am going to the Father* (John 14:12).

You literally and spiritually have been granted the same authority as Jesus to do His works on the earth. Jesus declared that sickness and disease are oppressions of the Devil and that is why healing was a major mandate of His ministry.

Luke wrote in the book of Acts,

> *How God anointed Jesus of Nazareth with the Holy Spirit and with power, and how Jesus went around doing good and healing all who were oppressed by the devil, because God was with Him* (Acts 10:38).

If you are afflicted with any form of sickness or disease, it is not from God. He is not trying to teach you something through it, for it is an oppression of the Devil. The same anointing Jesus had to heal and deliver others and even you is within you. It is released through faith in His mighty name – the name of Jesus!

Go and do what Jesus promised you could and would do. You honor Him with your faith when you act on His Word.

Prayer

Lord, make me an instrument of Your healing power. Awaken my heart to believe You for the healing of others and for my life and health. Touch my tongue so that it too will be loosed to pray for others and proclaim Your name. Touch my ears, and give me a hearing heart that I can discern Your voice and do the works of God. In Jesus' name, I pray.

Declaration

I declare that within my spirit is the DNA of God. I was created in His image and have been born again as a child of God. Therefore, I can do the works of God by the Holy Spirit who dwells within me. I declare that when I pray for healing, it will take place. When I rebuke the oppression of the Devil, it must flee, and when I proclaim the good news of Jesus, I too will see His power in my words.

> *Truly I tell you, whatever you bind on earth will be bound in heaven, and whatever you loose on earth will be loosed in heaven.*
> *Again, I tell you truly that if two of you on the earth agree about anything you ask for, it will be done for you by My Father in heaven. For where two or three gather together in My name, there am I with them* (Matthew 18:18-20).

Day 20

A Man Born Blind Is Healed

The unconventionality of the ministry of Jesus gives perspective to those who minister in healing and to those who are seeking healing. It teaches us not to close our thoughts or our eyes to the Lord's extraordinary methods and actions.

"Here's to Mud in Your Eye"

> *Now as Jesus was passing by, He saw a man blind from birth, and His disciples asked Him, "Rabbi, who sinned, this man or his parents, that he was born blind?"*
> *Jesus answered, "Neither this man nor his parents sinned, but this happened so that the works of God would be displayed in him. While it is daytime, we must do the works of Him who sent Me. Night is coming, when no one can work. While I am in the world, I am the light of the world."*
> *When Jesus had said this, He spat on the ground, made some mud, and applied it to the man's eyes. Then He told him, "Go, wash in the pool of*

Siloam" (which means Sent). So the man went and washed, and came back seeing.
At this, his neighbors and those who had formerly seen him begging began to ask, "Isn't this the man who used to sit and beg?"
Some claimed that he was, but others said, "No, he just looks like him."
But the man kept saying, "I am the one."
"How then were your eyes opened?" they asked.
He answered, "The man they call Jesus made some mud and anointed my eyes, and He told me to go to Siloam and wash. So I went and washed and received my sight"
(John 9:1-11).

They brought to the Pharisees the man who had been blind. Now the day on which Jesus had made the mud and opened his eyes was a Sabbath. So the Pharisees also asked him how he had received his sight. The man answered, "He put mud on my eyes, and I washed, and now I can see."
Because of this, some of the Pharisees said, "This man is not from God, for He does not keep the Sabbath" (John 9:13-16).

> *When Jesus heard that they had thrown him out, He found the man and said, "Do you believe in the Son of Man?"*
> *"Who is He, Sir?" he replied. "Tell me so that I may believe in Him."*
> *"You have already seen Him," Jesus answered. "He is the One speaking with you."*
> *"Lord, I believe," he said. And he worshiped Jesus.*
> *Then Jesus declared, "For judgment I have come into this world, so that the blind may see and those who see may become blind."*
> *Some of the Pharisees who were with Him heard this, and they asked Him, "Are we blind too?"*
> *"If you were blind," Jesus replied, "you would not be guilty of sin. But since you claim you can see, your guilt remains"* (John 9:35-41).

The entire Chapter of John 9 is devoted to this story of a man who was born blind and the unusual way Jesus healed him. This man's story began with a conversation that Jesus had with His disciples, and it took place right in front of the young man. As we have discussed in other parts of this book, the prevailing belief of the people at that time was that any deformity, sickness or disease a person was afflicted with was the result of the person's sin or that of the parents. What is striking about this dialogue is that it was coming from the Lord's own disciples. They had seen Jesus continually heal people out of a heart of mercy and compassion. Yet, they are the ones who posed the question. With every act of lovingkindness that was expressed in healing through the Lord's ministry, His disciples still did not make the connection to the truth about God's heart for His people.

The very way in which they asked the question revealed that this belief was embedded in their thinking. When the blind man heard that conversation, he might have been thinking about the disciples' insensitive assertion, "Hello, I'm standing right here. I may be blind, but I'm not deaf." It seems sad to say, but in this story, Jesus was not only restoring that man's eyes but also his dignity by saying that this situation would bring glory to God. But there's more: it was also about Jesus tearing down the negative belief that paints God as being a harsh, vindictive and even cruel God. Jesus was revealing the truth about the Father by His words and deeds. Those actions were meant to tear down the false images and with them, the indignity placed upon the Father.

Then, Jesus did something that seemed to be outlandish and even insulting to the man. He picked up some dirt, spat on it, made some mud and placed it on the man's eyes. It is a good thing that the man was blind because if he could have seen what this complete stranger was about to do, he might have assaulted Jesus as an act of self-defence. Jesus smeared the mud made from the dirt and His spittle on the man's face.

Jesus told His disciples that God's glory was about to be revealed. They must have also stood in shock as they watched Him put His mud on the man's eyes. And, in what must have appeared as adding insult to injury, the Lord told the man to go wash it off at the pool of Siloam. That blind man had to make his way through the streets of Jerusalem to get to the pool of Siloam to wash the mud from his eyes. This whole situation begged the question: what was going on there? On the surface, it appeared to be abuse to a physically challenged person.

Several things were in motion during those exchanges between the Lord and His disciples and also with the blind man. As the man heard Jesus speak, it was tearing down the belief that his blindness was because he was under the judgment of God. Those words planted hope in the man, and it began to grow. Then when he heard that the glory of God was going to be seen in his condition, faith was being awakened. Jesus spoke words of life that penetrated his heart with hope. Even at that point, he still did not know who was behind the voice that was speaking those most wonderful words.

Jesus was about to perform a miracle by recreating the man's eyes. Just like the day Adam was formed from the dust of the earth, Jesus took the dust of the earth and infused it with the DNA of God. That mud was placed on those eyes, and the Lord's DNA in His spittle was held in place by the mudpack. The time it took to wash off mud at that pool was the precise time necessary for that creative miracle to complete its work.

That man had never seen a single day in his life. He did not know what it was like to see. He lived in a world of darkness, only being able to distinguish things by sound and touch. He heard the voice of God and was touched by Him, but had no clue what He looked like. He later met the person behind the voice face-to-face. That man went from hearing Jesus and perceiving Him as just a man, to thinking that Jesus was a prophet. He completed his faith when he saw Jesus and worshiped Him as the Son of God.

If this man had ever imagined what his healing would look like, I think it is safe to say he would never have envisioned what took place. I guess when he gathered with his family for that celebration meal, a fitting toast might have been, "Here's to mud in your eyes!" Another creative miracle had taken place by the Lord using the most unconventional means to do it.

Therefore, keep your heart open: for you never know how God may want to heal your body. Listen to the voice of Jesus through His Word, as well as His Holy Spirit, and you will see the glory of God manifest miraculously in your life. However it comes, embrace it by faith.

Prayer

Lord, I ask You to help me recognize Your voice when You are speaking. Whether it is through Your Word, Your servants or in the stillness of my heart and thoughts, help me to hear Your voice. When I perceive that You are speaking to me, give me the courage to act upon what I believe You are asking me to do. Thank You, Lord, for my healing. In Jesus' name, I pray.

Declaration

I declare that my eyes are open to perceive and understand what You are doing in my life. I thank You Lord that I am not under judgment, but I am one who will see Your glory manifest in my life. Your words of life are health to my flesh; therefore, my body cannot be denied from receiving Your healing virtue. In Jesus' name, I am healed and have been made whole. Amen and thank You, Lord.

> *I, the LORD, have called you for a righteous purpose, and I will take hold of your hand.*
> *I will keep you and appoint you to be a covenant for the people and a light to the nations, to open the eyes of the blind, to bring prisoners out of the dungeon, and those sitting in darkness out from the prison house* (Isaiah 42:6-7, a prophecy concerning Jesus).

Day 21

Double Prayer to Cure Double Vision

This is the third time we read of Jesus using His DNA in the process of healing an individual.

The Healing of the Blind Man at Bethsaida

> *When they arrived at Bethsaida, some people brought a blind man and begged Jesus to touch him. So He took the blind man by the hand and led him out of the village. Then He spit on the man's eyes and placed His hands on him. "Can you see anything?" He asked.*
> *The man looked up and said, "I can see the people, but they look like trees walking around."*
> *Once again Jesus placed His hands on the man's eyes, and when he opened them his sight was restored, and he could see everything clearly. Jesus sent him home and said, "Do not go back into the village"* (Mark 8:22-26).

Bethsaida was not an easy place for Jesus to carry on His ministry. When the Lord began performing healings and miracles in that town, the people marveled and praised God for what they had witnessed. But then the people began to reason among themselves that Jesus couldn't be the Messiah because some of them knew His family. They reasoned that surely, the Messiah would not come from such humble means. With that kind of reasoning, it wasn't very long before He was accused of operating in the power of the Devil. Hence, it came as no surprise that after Jesus healed the man in this story, He told him not to return to the town or tell them what had happened.

> *Woe to you, Chorazin! Woe to you, Bethsaida! For if the miracles that were performed in you had happened in Tyre and Sidon, they would have repented long ago, sitting in sackcloth and ashes. But it will be more bearable at the judgment for Tyre and Sidon than for you* (Luke 10:13, 14).

I See People as Trees Walking Around

Here again was another example of people taking up the causes of loved ones and bringing them to Jesus for healing. What is so interesting about this story is the first thing that Jesus did. He led the man out of that town before ministering to him. Bethsaida had a faith-dousing atmosphere because of the unbelief of its inhabitants; therefore it was a difficult place to minister. The Greek word *proseuché* is the commonly translated word for prayer in English. It holds within its meaning the idea of an atmosphere or an environment of prayer. No atmosphere of prayer was to be found in that town.

Jesus purposely led the man out of that town and away from the unbelief of the crowd. The Lord would again use His DNA and place it on the man's eyes. Then He asked him what he saw. The man acknowledged that he had some degree of eyesight, but everything was blurred and presumably, not because of the spit. Jesus laid His hands on the man's eyes for a second time, and the healing was completed.

Two significant events took place in this story that we can all learn from. This is apart from the DNA we discussed in the two previous devotions. The first is that we read of no prayer being said over the person. The Bible speaks of the laying on of hands as an act of faith that transfers God's power. It is as if the person's touch acts as a conduit to the ailing person. In Mark Chapter 16, we read as part of the Great Commission the command to lay hands on the sick, and they will recover. This act was as much a part of prayer as any words would be.

The second thing we can draw from this man's testimony is that we should not stop believing or ministering until the job is complete. Not every healing is immediate or instantaneous. Sometimes the healing may take gradual progression or simply require an additional act of prayer. Don't be discouraged during the healing process and never take your faith off .your healing. Do not base your beliefs solely on what you see because your healing may come as a process or in stages. What may be a blur now is just one step closer to the completion of your healing. If the Lord had to act twice as He did in this man's story, we should be bold to keep on moving forward in faith and continue to pray as often as necessary.

Healings can be as immediate and dramatic as the testimonies that we are reading about in this devotional or they can be gradual. Jesus gave us many examples that likened the workings of the kingdom of God to a seed and its development.

> *Jesus also said, "The kingdom of God is like a man who scatters seed on the ground. Night and day he sleeps and wakes, and the seed sprouts and grows, though he knows*

> *not how. All by itself the earth produces a crop—first the stalk, then the head, then grain that ripens within. And as soon as the grain is ripe, he swings the sickle, because the harvest has come"* (Mark 4:26-29).

There is an unseen progression of every seed of faith that is sown, and that picture that Jesus paints is relevant to any person of any generation or age. Some people's harvest seasons may be short, while others may run their course through the entire crop-growing season. Do not lose heart by what you see or don't see, feel or not feel because the first part of the growth is unseen. If a farmer went into his field every day and dug up his seed to see if it was growing, I don't know that the seed would ever break open and grow. So in like manner, keep on trusting God that what you have believed for has taken place, and you will eventually see the evidence of your faith.

At the end of the devotional section of this book, I have added supplemental teaching on the subject of the kingdom of God. Jesus used the nature of the seed and its growth to describe how His kingdom functions. It is helpful for our understanding of how healing takes place.

Prayer

Heavenly Father, I ask for wisdom to understand what You are doing in my life and to discern Your timing. You said in Your Word that You will provide seed for the sower, so I receive each scriptural promise of healing as my personal seed. Thank You for this seed, and I ask You to bring forth a bountiful crop of answers to my prayers. In Jesus' name.

Declaration

I am not moved by what I see or feel. I am only moved by what I believe. Therefore, I declare that no matter how long it takes to complete my healing, I will see it through to victory. My body responds with healing to the life-giving words of my Lord Jesus that I confess on my lips. Jesus said that faith has the inherent power to move mountains, so in the name of Jesus, I command my mountain of trouble to be cast into the sea. I believe that these words will come to pass. The victory is mine. Amen.

> *We want each of you to show the same diligence to the very end, so that your hope may be fully assured. Then you will not be sluggish, but will imitate those who through faith and patience inherit*

what has been promised (Hebrews 6:11, 12).

Day 22

When Unbelief Is a Perversion

It is important to understand that unbelief in God is an indirect way of saying that you believe He is not able to meet your need. I have combined two accounts of the boy's deliverance from the Gospels to give a more detailed look into the story.

The Deliverance of the Boy with Seizures

> *When they returned to the other disciples, they saw a large crowd around them and scribes arguing with them. As soon as all the people saw Jesus, they were filled with awe and ran to greet Him.*
> *"What are you disputing with them?" He asked.*
> *Someone in the crowd replied, "Teacher, I brought You my son, who has a spirit that makes him mute. Whenever it seizes him, it throws him to the ground. He foams at the mouth, gnashes his teeth, and becomes rigid. I asked Your disciples to drive it out, but they were unable."*

*"O unbelieving generation!" Jesus replied. "How long must I remain with you? How long must I put up with you? Bring the boy to Me."
So they brought him, and seeing Jesus, the spirit immediately threw the boy into a convulsion. He fell to the ground and rolled around, foaming at the mouth.
Jesus asked the boy's father, "How long has this been with him?"
"From childhood," he said. "It often throws him into the fire or into the water, trying to kill him. But if You can do anything, have compassion on us and help us."
"If You can?" echoed Jesus. "All things are possible to him who believes!"
Immediately the boy's father cried out, "I do believe; help my unbelief!"
When Jesus saw that a crowd had come running, He rebuked the unclean spirit. "You deaf and mute spirit," He said, "I command you to come out and never enter him again."
After shrieking and convulsing him violently, the spirit came out. The boy became like a corpse, so that many said, "He is dead." But Jesus took him by the hand and helped him*

to his feet, and he stood up* (Mark 9:14-27).

When they came to the crowd, a man came up to Jesus and knelt before Him. "Lord, have mercy on my son," he said. "He has seizures and is suffering terribly. He often falls into the fire or into the water. I brought him to Your disciples, but they could not heal him."
"O unbelieving and perverse generation!" Jesus replied. "How long must I remain with you? How long must I put up with you? Bring the boy here to Me." Then Jesus rebuked the demon, and it came out of the boy, and he was healed from that moment.
Afterward the disciples came to Jesus privately and asked, "Why couldn't we drive it out?"
"Because you have so little faith." He answered. "For truly I tell you, if you have faith the size of a mustard seed, you can say to this mountain, 'Move from here to there,' and it will move. Nothing will be impossible for you" (Matthew 17:14-20).

When Unbelief Is a Perversion

Before we delve into this powerful report, let me give you a bit of a backdrop to what you have just read.

Jesus had taken His three trusted disciples, Peter, James, and John with Him up into the mountain for prayer. The remaining disciples stayed in a nearby town for the night until the Lord met them the following day. In the morning, Jesus and His three disciples returned from the mountain, and it was there that they encountered a chaotic situation in that town. A man whose child was demonized had approached the disciples who remained behind. He asked them if they could deliver his child from his torment. As much as they tried, the boy received no relief from his suffering and the convulsions continued. That dramatic scene drew a crowd of spectators and shortly thereafter, the disciples found themselves in a heated argument with some of the religious leaders who came to see what was going on. It was then that a religious debate ensued as to why they couldn't heal the boy, which only added to the furor. That was the backdrop to the story as Jesus appeared on the scene.

You can imagine what a spectacle it must have been once the father of the child recognized that Jesus had arrived. The attention now turned to the Lord as the man and the crowd made a beeline to Him.

Immediately, the Lord took control of the situation and calmed everyone down. He asked the father of the child what had happened, to which the father told Jesus that His disciples were powerless to help his son. He then asked the Lord if He could do something. "If"? It is to that response that Jesus made an indictment on that entire generation by calling it unbelieving and perverse.

Why did the Lord make such a strong accusation against His generation? Why did the word "if" create such a response from Jesus? Well, the nation had long moved away from trusting in God. Religion had become a cultural formality. They lived in such a way that God was given mere lip service when it came to being involved in their lives. I wonder if the Lord would say any less about our generation because it certainly seems similar to how we live.

Nothing about this scenario would be a Faith Hall of Fame moment. It wasn't so for the disciples or the parent of the child, and it certainly wasn't for the crowd or the religious leaders who turned the entire situation into a spectacle of arguments and confusion. Jesus called a spade, a spade. The word perversion means to alter something from its original meaning or state. It is a distortion or corruption of what was originally intended. To believe that a demon's power was greater than God's power was perversion of the highest order. That is why the Lord gave such an angry response. The man probably didn't realize that questioning the Lord's power to deliver his child was an implication that Satan had more power to do evil than God had power to do good.

It was at that moment that the man cried out, *"I believe, help my unbelief."*
Those words are the pleas of the downtrodden, those who have been beaten down by the circumstances they have to endure. It was in that moment of honesty that the Lord was given something to work with. The man first approached the Lord blaming His disciples and then questioned the Lord's power. It was only after Jesus challenged his words that he finally acknowledged his unbelief.

As weak as we may feel in our crises of life, Jesus will meet us at any point if we come to Him in humility. Nothing in our thoughts or beliefs surprises the Lord, so it is better to simply be honest with God. That man tried to shift the blame; it was only after the Lord called him out that he came clean. It was then that Jesus cast the demon out of the child and returned him healed to his father.

The central issue in all of these testimonies of healing is that the successful results always come through faith. Whether it is the Lord using His faith as in this day's devotional, the faith of others or your own faith in Jesus, faith releases the power of God. It triggers the opening of the floodgates of His kingdom, and it is never absent of the Lord's faith-filled agreement with our prayers. This whole episode became a teaching moment for the disciples, and the Lord ended His instruction by saying nothing is impossible to anyone who believes. Even if it appears to be the smallest amount of faith, Jesus makes the impossible possible. You may feel that all you can offer is your meager trickle of faith, but it will invite the Lord to join it to His vast river of faith and power in partnership with you.

Prayer

Heavenly Father, I humble myself to You this day. Cleanse my heart of any trace of unbelief that would question Your power or ability. Give me an understanding of the depths of love and favor You have for me, so that my trust in You will not falter or be swayed. Make Your truth come alive in me, so I will always be able to stand before you and say, "I believe." In Jesus' name I offer this prayer.

Declaration

I believe all things are possible for me because I believe in Jesus and His Word. With every scripture I read that says something is possible for them, I make that same word my possibility. I believe when I agree with God's Word, God is agreeing with me, which means I can do all things through Christ who strengthens me. All of the benefits of salvation are mine in Christ. I am saved, healed, delivered, and provided for by God until the day I go home to be with my God. I declare it as my inheritance in Jesus. Amen.

> *Call upon Me in the day of trouble; I will deliver you, and you will honor Me* (Psalm 50:15).

> *Humble yourselves before the Lord, and He will exalt you* (James 4:10).

Day 23

And Jesus Healed Them All

When a person experiences healing or a miracle, it helps others to believe. It awakens hope and encouragement, which takes them just one step of faith away from a miracle of their own.

The Contagion of Faith

> *When they had crossed over, they landed at Gennesaret. And when the men of that place recognized Jesus, they sent word to all the surrounding region. People brought all the sick to Him, and begged Him just to let them touch the fringe of His cloak. And all who touched Him were healed* (Matthew 14:34-36).

> *Moving on from there, Jesus went along the Sea of Galilee. Then He went up on a mountain and sat down. Large crowds came to Him, bringing the lame, the blind, the crippled, the mute, and many others, and laid them at His feet, and He healed them. The crowd was amazed when they saw the mute speaking,*

the crippled restored, the lame walking, and the blind seeing. And they glorified the God of Israel (Matthew 15:29-31).

Then Jesus came down with them and stood on a level place. A large crowd of His disciples was there, along with a great number of people from all over Judea, Jerusalem, and the sea coast of Tyre and Sidon. They had come to hear Him and to be healed of their diseases, and those troubled by unclean spirits were healed. The entire crowd was trying to touch Him, because power was coming from Him and healing them all (Luke 6:17-19).

These three passages you have just read are from three different events that were recorded. It tells us that healing became a common occurrence under the Lord's ministry. It also shows us that there were times when all those who needed miracles became enveloped in that atmosphere of faith and received their healing. That is astounding and almost unthinkable to the religious minds because they would reason that there had to be disqualified people in any given crowd. Someone must be in sin, strife or some other violation that would place him or her outside of God's goodness and grace.

Well, there was a disqualification for someone not to be healed by Jesus. In Matthew Chapter 13, which was just before the passage that started today's devotional, we read this concerning Jesus:

> *Coming to His hometown, He taught the people in their synagogue, and they were astonished. "Where did this man get such wisdom and miraculous powers?" they asked. "Is this not the carpenter's son? Isn't His mother's name Mary, and aren't His brothers James, Joseph, Simon, and Judas? Aren't all His sisters with us as well? Where then did this man get all these things?" And they took offense at Him.*
> *But Jesus said to them, "Only in his hometown and in his own household is a prophet without honor." **And He did not do many miracles there, because of their unbelief*** (Matthew 13:54-58).

Unbelief was the sole disqualification from healing in the Lord's ministry. Having said that, it still did not stop His merciful kindness from being released as we have read often in these devotional teachings.

Think about those crowds of people for a moment. Do you really think they were all perfectly righteous and had their lives in order? Of course not, religion tries to fix you first in order to make you a worthy candidate for God's favor. However, Jesus loves you as you are and gives His gifts freely. Then He gives you His righteousness as a gift of grace.

Can you imagine how the rest of the people's faith was affected when one person was miraculously healed in a crowd? It created a firestorm of belief that furthered the release of more of God's power. Only believe! There is no precondition on this crowd in any way. It was solely a matter of their belief in Jesus the healer. If we stop to examine the heart condition of that crowd, what might we see? I am certain that it would represent a cross-section of a town like yours. You would have every kind of sin represented in that crowd and every commandment being broken. Yet, this did not deter a single person from being healed by Jesus on that day.

God's mercy triumphs over judgment; that is His heart to every lost or wayward soul and to all who know Him. Also, consider what those miracles would have meant to the families of those who were healed. Think about the impact on the communities of those people who were healed under Jesus' ministry. There were no hospitals or government care; all those ailing relied on their families, friends or possibly communities to assist them. The healing ministry of Jesus lifted the burden of care off the entire region and gave His rest to all who provided care. Consider the emotional, physical, and financial weight carried by families whose loved ones are ailing. No words of praise are sufficient to offer God when Jesus touches a community. He changes everything and brings rest to all who would receive Him.

You may be in a crowd of one at home or in a hospital bed, but know this: you are beloved of God. His voice is still speaking through His Word today. He is saying to you: "Fear not; only believe." Your miracle may be the catalyst to start a firestorm of healing in your city or community.

Prayer

Dear Lord, I bring my life before You, and I ask that Your grace be poured over my wounds and infirmities as a healing ointment. I reach out to You by faith to touch the hem of Your garment, and I believe You for my healing in Jesus' name I pray. Amen.

Declaration

Father, I thank You that Your Word is true, and I humbly claim that I do believe. I thank You in advance for the complete restoration of my health. I am healed. I am sick no longer, for I know that it is Your good pleasure to give me Your kingdom. There are no sicknesses in heaven, so I believe it is Your will on earth for me as it is in heaven. Thank You, Lord. I declare this in the mighty name of Jesus.

> *But seek His kingdom, and these things will be added unto you. Do not be afraid, little flock, for your Father is pleased to give you the kingdom* (Luke 12:31, 32).

Day 24

One Funeral - Two Raised from the Dead

No matter what you may be facing in your life or that of a loved one, if the situation seems hopeless, today's devotional was written for you.

Jesus Raises a Widow's Son

> *Soon afterward, Jesus went to a town called Nain. His disciples went with Him, accompanied by a large crowd. As He approached the town gate, He saw a dead man being carried out, the only son of his mother, and she was a widow. And a sizeable crowd from the town was with her.*
> *When the Lord saw her, He had compassion on her and said, "Do not weep." Then He went up and touched the coffin, and those carrying it stood still. "Young man," He said, "I tell you, get up!" And the dead man sat up and began to speak! Then Jesus gave him back to his mother.*
> *A sense of awe swept over all of them, and they glorified God. "A*

> *great prophet has appeared among us!" they said. "God has visited His people!" And the news about Jesus spread throughout Judea and all the surrounding region* (Luke 7:11-17).

This woman's story had all the makings of a tragic tale; it was one of sorrow and heartbreak. We learn that she had already experienced pain and loss because of the death of her husband; now, her only son had died. Stricken with grief, she walked in the funeral procession that was taking her adult son outside of the town for his burial. With every step she took, the weight of her sorrow seemed like ten thousand pounds on her shoulders that day. Her desperate pleas to God to save her son, in her mind, had gone unnoticed. If faith and hope could be accounted to her as a currency, then as far as that goes, she spent all she had in those prayers for her son.

As stated before, when tragedies like this occurred, the prevailing thought in her day was that God was judging her or her son for some committed sin. It makes one wonder what her thoughts about God must have been in the midst of her mourning and loss. When she lost her husband and provider, the responsibility for her well-being was placed on her son. Now, he was gone and she faced a very uncertain future – quite possibly, one that would find her all alone. If through her tears she begged God that she too would die, would anyone have thought less of her?

Just as she and much of the town were heading out the gate, Jesus was about to enter that town. The Lord fixed His eyes on her and with great love and compassion, He brought the funeral march to a stop. One brief sentence is recorded as being said by Jesus to the woman; it was, "Don't cry." Through those caring simple words, life would shatter the pall of death. Some think the two most compelling words in the New Testament are "Jesus wept." But I think it was when He said to that heartbroken woman, "Don't cry." Why? Because He was about to turn her world upside down in a dramatic way. Jesus spoke to her dead son who immediately sat up, and He returned him to his mother. One can only imagine the kind of celebration that must have occurred in that family and town after that young man was raised from the dead. A great defeat was turned into a great victory all because Jesus made a visit to that town called, Nain.

It is worth noting that Jesus did not ask the woman to believe, for I am certain He already knew her heart was spent. He did not ask her to repent or jump through any of the religious hoops that people believe have to be followed as a formula for God to act.

No. All He cared about in that moment was ending her suffering, so He asked her not to cry and then He showed her why.

Life happens when Jesus intervenes in our times of trouble and even death cannot bear His presence. There is no situation so grave, no moment of time unnoticed, no faint, desperate plea so quiet that it will escape our Lord's attention.

Someone might look at this death and say, "God's timing had failed them" but to that dear woman who just happened to cross the Lord's path, His timing was perfect as the end result shows. By coming at that last critical moment of time, Jesus not only gave her back her son, He also gave her the belief that nothing is impossible with God. No matter what she might face in the future, she had an unshakeable foundation of faith in God's goodness and care for her well-being.

Even in your darkest hour, a rendezvous with the God of heaven is just a moment away. He will enter your situation and supply your needs. If this event in the widow's life had happened five minutes sooner or later, the outcome would have been different. The God who loves you and knows your need is there for you just as He was for that widow. Even when something you value dearly appears to have died, it is not out of the realm of His compassion and resurrection power. Allow these words to enter your heart. Let them bring you courage and strength to stand firm in the knowledge that a miracle is at the gate.

Prayer

Father, I thank You for what You did for that woman. I believe You have the same heart towards me. I am going to stop my tears in the expectation that You have answered my prayer. I will trust You and believe that no time is too late to see a miraculous demonstration of Your power in my life. In Jesus' name.

Declaration

I declare in Jesus' name that premature death will not destroy my life or my destiny in God. Jesus Christ has made me alive, and that truth will permeate every area of my life. This speaks to my hopes given by God, inspired dreams, prophetic words, and the promises found in the Word of God. All the things promised in salvation: healing, deliverance, provision, safety, and well-being are mine in Jesus' name until I go home to heaven to be with Him there.

Be merciful to me, O LORD, for I am frail; heal me, O LORD, for my bones are in agony.
My soul is deeply distressed. How long, O LORD, how long?
Turn, O LORD, and deliver my soul; save me because of Your loving devotion.
For there is no mention of You in death; who can praise You from Sheol? (Psalm 6:2-5).
Jesus answered, "I am the way, the truth, and the life. No one comes to the Father except through Me (John 14:6).

Day 25

When It's the Wrong Time to be Lending Your Ear

I am sure we've all heard the quote, "Friends, Romans, countrymen, lend me your ears," which is the first line of a speech by Mark Antony in the play, "Julius Caesar" by William Shakespeare. Of all the testimonies of healing in the Gospels, this one by far has the most unusual dynamic found in its story. I am asking you to lend me your ears and hear God's Word, which brings faith for healing. Malchus offered no ear in any way or at any time and got his ear healed by the God of mercy. If he was a candidate for healing, then most certainly, so are you.

Malchus

> *While Jesus was still speaking, Judas, one of the Twelve, arrived, accompanied by a large crowd armed with swords and clubs, sent from the chief priests and elders of the people.*
> *Now the betrayer had arranged a signal with them: "The one I kiss is the man; arrest Him." Going directly*

> to Jesus, he said, "Greetings, Rabbi," and kissed Him.
> "Friend," Jesus replied, "do what you came for."
> Then the men stepped forward, seized Jesus, and arrested Him. At this, one of Jesus' companions drew his sword and struck the servant of the high priest, cutting off his ear.
> "Put your sword back in its place," Jesus said to him. "For all who draw the sword will die by the sword. Are you not aware that I can call on My Father, and He will at once put at my disposal more than twelve legions of angels? But how then would the Scriptures be fulfilled that say it must happen this way?"
> At that time Jesus said to the crowd, "Have you come out with swords and clubs to arrest Me as you would an outlaw? Every day I sat teaching in the temple courts, and you did not arrest Me. But this has all happened so that the writings of the prophets would be fulfilled"

(Matthew 26:47-56).

An Unwitting Victim of Healing

This event took place the day before Jesus was crucified and just after He spent the evening with His disciples to celebrate the Passover meal. It was shortly afterward that

Judas left and went to the religious authorities to give them the location where the Lord was staying. This was the moment they were waiting for. They had sought for a time when they could arrest Jesus in a private place because they feared if He was arrested in the open, the people of Jerusalem might rise up against them. However, they had their opportunity this time because the streets were mostly clear as families remained together at home celebrating. This would have been the ideal time to arrest Jesus in relative secrecy. The plans were put in place, and the soldiers were readied as they waited for word from Judas about the Lord's location. He would lead them to Jesus with a large contingent of the temple guards along with many of the leaders and their supporters armed with swords and clubs. Finally, they would get their hands on the one they believed to be a false prophet and a troublemaker who upset the status quo of their nation.

Chaos erupted when Judas betrayed Jesus with a kiss. That was the sign to identify Him to the soldiers so they could arrest Him. Peter had envisioned they would all go down fighting and grabbed a sword (which was more like a large dagger). He struck and severed the ear of a man named Malchus. He was the servant of the high priest and was probably part of the lead group that arrested the Lord. Jesus quickly stopped His disciples from taking any further action and ended the situation by surrendering Himself to the mob. In what must have seemed like a surreal moment, before things would go any further, the Lord picked up the ear of Malchus and healed him right in the middle of that intense scene.

The Anti-Belief of Malchus

Most of the religious authorities deeply despised Jesus and viewed him as a threat to their rule and their peace with Rome. In that environment of hatred, Malchus was probably no different from any of the other voices that spoke ill of Jesus over the course of the Lord's ministry among them. If Malchus believed anything, it was probably that his arrest was the best thing that could happen in an already tense and increasingly hostile situation with their Roman occupiers. For all of his disregard of Jesus and dismissal of Him as a prophet or the Messiah, he experienced the Lord's touch and was impacted by the healing power of God. For Malchus, this was not merely a question of unbelief; his was a full-blown case of anti-belief. So how does he qualify for healing from God? Well, the simple answer is that he didn't qualify. The issue was not about his hate; rather, it was about the Lord's love.

That evening in the garden of Gethsemane marked one of the most sorrowful moments of the Lord's life on earth. During His time of prayer that night, he saw and experienced in His Spirit, what He would soon be living out in the coming hours. He saw it all, the betrayal, the denials, the beatings, and His eventual death, but none of that had created any hatred in Him. Instead, when He saw Malchus hunched over and bleeding from Peter's assault, He had compassion on him and healed him. There was no faith reaching out to the Lord from Malchus; there were no friends acting as intercessors on his behalf. The man's healing was solely by the mercy and compassion of Jesus extended to the very one who hated Him. As Jesus was bound and led away as a criminal, I wonder what Malchus was thinking? How could a man accused of being possessed by the Devil show him that kind of mercy and do such a miracle for him? I would think that those thoughts would have haunted him as he tried to reconcile all that had happened on that night.

How do we process a story such as this? How do we find a teaching example we can apply to our lives? There is a purpose to this story for us. It is to show that no matter what a person believes about Jesus or how much hostility he holds against Him; he is never far from His tender mercy and lovingkindness. Jesus will love you, seek to find you in your deepest pit of hell, and restore you to His Father in heaven. Even if you have nothing to offer Him, He offers you everything through His life. This was the last healing by Jesus that was recorded in the New Testament. I believe it was written so that all those in need, no matter what they previously believed about Jesus, can know they are never far from His mercy and grace. This last testimony of healing was solely an act of the Lord's mercy and is the fitting completion of His healing message to the world. He is the answer and the healer of all mankind to this very day. Wherever you are and in whatever mindset you are in, He will meet you at the crossroads. You are never as far from His grace as you might think or suppose.

Prayer

Lord, I thank You for the awesome love You have for me. I ask You to heal me, for I believe it is Your good pleasure to do so. Even if I had a mindset like that of Malchus, I would still be a candidate for healing solely because of Your mercy and compassion. I believe in Your love for me over any of my own beliefs, and I thank You for my healing and deliverance. In Jesus' name.

Declaration

Lord, I believe You are a God of great mercy and compassion. If Malchus can be healed, then so can I. Therefore, I speak to my body to be healed and restored to health and strength. In Jesus' name.

> *In them the prophecy of Isaiah is fulfilled: 'You will be ever hearing but never understanding; you will be ever seeing but never perceiving. For this people's heart has grown callous; they hardly hear with their ears,*
> *and they have closed their eyes. Otherwise they might see with their eyes, hear with their ears, understand with their hearts, and turn, and I would heal them.'*
> *But blessed are your eyes because they see, and your ears because they hear* (Matthew 13:14-16).

Day 26

Jesus Sends Out His Ministry Teams

Jesus prepared His disciple's to carry on His ministry after His ascension. He knew that His departure was soon coming, but His message and work were to continue as if He had never left. To do this, the Lord multiplied His outreach by sending out teams to proclaim His message of good news. They would go forth with the demonstration of the Spirit and power and see the healing virtue of Jesus released through their own ministry.

The remaining testimonies of healing in this devotional will now be seen through the eyes of the Lord's followers as they continued His work and will on the earth.

Jesus Commissions the Twelve

> *Jesus called His twelve disciples to Him and gave them authority over unclean spirits, to drive them out and to heal every disease and sickness. These are the names of the twelve apostles: first Simon, called Peter, and his brother Andrew; James son*

> of Zebedee, and his brother John; Philip and Bartholomew; Thomas and Matthew the tax collector; James son of Alphaeus, and Thaddaeus; Simon the Zealot, and Judas Iscariot, who betrayed Jesus. These twelve Jesus sent out with the following instructions: "Do not go onto the road of the Gentiles or enter any town of the Samaritans. Go rather to the lost sheep of Israel. As you go, preach this message: 'The kingdom of heaven is near.' Heal the sick, raise the dead, cleanse the lepers, drive out demons. Freely you have received; freely give* (Matthew 10:1-8).

Jesus Commissions 72 Disciples to Preach, Heal, and Deliver

> *After this, the Lord appointed seventy-two others and sent them two by two ahead of Him to every town and place He was about to visit. And He told them, "The harvest is plentiful, but the workers are few. Ask the Lord of the harvest, therefore, to send out workers into His harvest.
> Go! I am sending you out like lambs among wolves* (Luke 10:1-3).

Their Joyful Return

> *The seventy-two returned with joy and said, "Lord, even the demons submit to us in Your name."*
> *So He said to them, "I saw Satan fall like lightning from heaven. See, I have given you authority to tread on snakes and scorpions, and over all the power of the enemy. Nothing will harm you. Nevertheless, do not rejoice that the spirits submit to you, but rejoice that your names are written in heaven"* (Luke 10:17-20).

I have linked these passages together for the purpose of showing that the multiplication of the ministry of Jesus did not mean a weakening of His healing anointing. Both groups and the ministry teams that were formed carried out the Lord's mandate of Isaiah 61, which we have previously read about. Both groups followed the Lord's instructions and saw the same results of His power. We see the apostles doing great works, which we seem to readily accept as a given. But remember, even Judas was doing miracles as one who was numbered with the Twelve. Later, we read of the seventy-two mostly nameless individuals who were also given the same commission with the same powerful results.

How exciting it must have been for them to return and tell the Lord all the testimonies of His healing power that was at work through their ministry. Do you realize at that time none of the apostles or the seventy-two were born again? In other words, as believers, they were not new creations in Christ and had also not experienced the indwelling of the Holy Spirit. In fact, they were operating solely on the command of Jesus; the Holy Spirit was working with them but not in them. This was before the Lord went to the cross.

As a Christian today, you stand in a much higher place than they were at that time. Your redemption was made complete through the cross, and you have the promise of the Holy Spirit as your resident companion. You are now a joint-heir with Christ because of the gift of salvation that was made available to all through His cross. You can freely enjoy all of the benefits of being part of His family and have the right to use His name with authority.

What this means is that you have the same commission by Jesus to do His works and proclaim His Word with a demonstration of His power to your community. His Spirit is in you. His covenant of promise is inscribed on your heart, and you are a child of the King of kings and the Lord of Lords. You may be saying to yourself, "That can't be me; you don't know what I have done. I barely live like a Christian. How can I speak with authority and see His power work through my life?" Listen, never demean yourself before the Lord; it is an insult to Him. The gospel of Jesus Christ is not about you; it is all about Jesus and what He has done for you. When you speak negatively about yourself, you are implying that your perception of your value is greater than God's perception of who you are in Christ. He cherishes you and has the highest regard for and expectation of you, as well as who you are maturing into as a person.

Whenever I have a negative thought about myself and am about to speak ill of me, I have learned (most times) to capture it and be silent before I speak it out to the Lord. I do this to honor the Lord. It is not about ego or pride; it is about coming into agreement with your heavenly Father. It is a false humility in God's eyes to defame yourself or be self-deprecating. A true mark of humility is when you value God's opinion as greater than your own. I know that can be difficult at times because we see and have to live through the dumb things that we do or are capable of doing. Nevertheless, it requires the same faith to believe what I have just asked you to do as it does to believe anything else. That is why the gospel of

Jesus is unlike any religion in the world. Religion tells you to get right and then God will accept you. Jesus makes you righteous through His life and then walks with you, lives in you and helps you to reproduce His life through yours. Faith sees what is not seen and brings it into the seen realm. See yourself as the righteousness of God in Christ anointed to do His works, and you will live out that truth in your life.

The disciples simply obeyed the instructions of the Lord and saw signs and wonders accomplished through their ministry to others. Even when we lack any great faith, the fact that we can trust in His faith carries us to the goal. You can look at it from the perspective of this quote from Jesus,

> *Come to Me, all you who are weary and burdened, and I will give you rest. Take My yoke upon you and learn from Me; for I am gentle and humble in heart, and you will find rest for your souls. For My yoke is easy and My burden is light"*
> (Matthew 11:28-30).

Oxen are paired together in a yoke that joins them as a team when they furrow a field. The Lord tells us that if you join Him under His yoke, it will be less strenuous and the burden will be light. But why is that the case? The reason should be obvious to all of us because He will shoulder the load for us. If we would just do what He asks us to do from the scriptures and follow the leadings that He places on our hearts, the results will be His. We will then have the joy of knowing that we partnered with Him and have seen His power at work, even in our day.

Execute that spiritual authority granted to you by Jesus and demonstrate His power in your life and in the lives of others. To do this is to obey the Great Commission the Lord has given to all believers.

> *Then Jesus came to them and said, "All authority in heaven and on earth has been given to Me. Therefore go and make disciples of all nations, baptizing them in the name of the Father, and of the Son, and of the Holy Spirit, and teaching them to obey all that I have commanded you. And surely I am with you always, to the very end of the age"* (Matthew 28:18-20).

Prayer

Lord, I lay down every opinion that I held about myself that is contrary to what You believe about me. I know You dearly love me, and my righteousness does not come by trying to attain it through my works. It is solely based on Jesus Christ alone. Help me embed this truth into my heart that I can love myself and others as You have loved me. Thank You, Lord, for all You have done for us. In Your name, I offer this prayer of thanksgiving.

Declaration

I gladly lay down any opinion of myself that disagrees with God's opinion of me and declare I can do all things through Christ who strengthens me. I also declare Your truth over my life from John 4:17, which says, *"As He is so also are we in this world."* I will boldly minister the Word of God with signs following based on this verse of Scripture. I believe that Jesus answers every lack and every need for my life, my family, and my friends and to those I come in contact with. This is my declaration. In Jesus' name. Amen.

> *And He said to them, "Go into all the world and preach the gospel to every creature. Whoever believes and is baptized will be saved, but whoever does not believe will be condemned. And these signs will accompany those who believe: In My name they will drive out demons; they will speak in new tongues; they*

Jesus Sends Out His Ministry Teams

will pick up snakes with their hands, and if they drink any deadly poison, it will not harm them; they will lay their hands on the sick, and they will be made well" (Mark 16:15-18).

Day 27

Intercession in Action

The book of Proverbs says there are friends who stay closer than a brother. This is the biblical record of a group of believers who would not quit on their beloved friend's need for healing. Even after her death, they still believed and would not give in to death on her behalf.

The Raising of Dorcas from the Dead

> *As Peter traveled throughout the area, he went to visit the saints in Lydda. There he found a man named Aeneas, who had been paralyzed and bedridden for eight years. "Aeneas," Peter said to him, "Jesus Christ heals you! Get up and put away your mat." Immediately Aeneas got up, and all who lived in Lydda and Sharon saw him and turned to the Lord.*
>
> *In Joppa there was a disciple named Tabitha (which is translated as Dorcas), who was always occupied with works of kindness and charity. At that time, however, she*

became sick and died, and her body was washed and placed in an upper room. Since Lydda was near Joppa, the disciples heard that Peter was there and sent two men to urge him, "Come to us without delay."

So Peter got up and went with them. On his arrival, they took him to the upper room. All the widows stood around him, weeping and showing him the tunics and other clothing that Dorcas had made while she was still with them.

Then Peter sent them all out of the room. He knelt down and prayed, and turning toward her body, he said, "Tabitha, get up!" She opened her eyes, and seeing Peter, she sat up. Peter took her by the hand and helped her up. Then he called the saints and widows and presented her to them alive.

This became known all over Joppa, and many people believed in the Lord. And Peter stayed for several days in Joppa with a tanner named Simon (Acts 9:32-43).

Dorcas was a woman who believed in the Lord and had served her community with acts of charity that flowed from her heart of love. The Bible does not record what had befallen her but who knows? It might have been that in her service to the sick and afflicted, she too became ill and died.

Sometimes in situations like this, we try to make some sense of it all. We reason that the person had lived a full life and perhaps, it was just his or her time to go. Other times, we may grieve that it was far too soon for our loved ones to be taken from us, especially when it seems that their whole lives were still ahead of them. Whatever was going through the hearts and minds of her friends and family, there was one thing we can be sure of: they were unwilling to surrender their loved one to death. Her family and friends had prayed for her healing and believed for her recovery, but now, they were left to wonder why.

It was then they got word that Peter was in the area and hope began to rise in their hearts. They had heard of the miraculous being done through his ministry and went in search of him, so they could ask him to urgently come and pray for their loved one. They were determined to do for her, what she could no longer do for herself. Peter obliged their plea and they set out together for the town of Joppa. As each hour passed, thoughts of the finality of death increased in the minds of those believers who were at the bedside of their friend. Their eyes had not betrayed what seemed to be the only reality to that sad state of affairs. If there was a faint breath or a weak pulse, it would have been something to hang on to, but now, what hope they had faded under the overwhelming evidence of the circumstances.

When Peter arrived, he found that the friends and family had gone into mourning and were grieving the loss of their loved one. They eulogized her life to Peter, telling him of all the wonderful traits and acts that made up the life of that dear woman. It was the faith of those friends who first sought Peter, and it was faith that rose up in Peter and compelled him to come. But that environment of faith had rapidly faded. As Peter read the situation, his response would be the key to seeing that woman raised from the dead. When we find ourselves in crises, the prevailing thought of our day is to get as many people praying as possible. We might all join hands and raise our voices up to God in prayer, thinking that strength comes in numbers. But Peter thought differently; after all, he was a close associate of the Lord Jesus and was one of the three disciples Jesus always took with Him in situations just like this one.

Peter quickly assessed and discerned what needed to be done. Those dear believers had spent all of the energy of their faith bringing

Peter to Dorcas. But now, there was no more fuel in the tank. Who could fault them? The overwhelming reality of the facts they faced had exhausted their supply of faith. Peter knew that their grieving had affected their faith and it would be better to pray alone, rather than ask them to join him. An atmosphere of faith was essential to see the release of God's miraculous power. Peter remembered how Jesus handled a similar situation when they had gone to the home of Jairus and witnessed his daughter being raised from the dead. The Lord had removed all of the sorrowful and unbelieving from the room on that day, and Peter would do the same. He wasted no time; he asked everyone to leave the room before he started to pray. The words of Jesus were probably resounding in his spirit saying, "All things are possible to him who believes." With that, the man of God took action and commanded Dorcas to get up. At that moment, a man rose from his knees and helped a woman who was brought back to life to rise to her feet.

Words of life are released with power when they come from those who offer prayer on bended knees.

Jesus is the resurrection and the life and no medical diagnosis is the final authority because all power and authority reside in

Him. It took a prayer of faith coming from one believer to transform death to life. God is no respecter of persons. His delight is found in anyone who would dare to believe Him; nothing is out of the reach of His power.

Friends may have interceded on your behalf asking the Lord to act. In doing so, they have faithfully brought you to the one who is the answer. Now, you too can be a Peter to your own Dorcas situation, and you too can see God's power bring life to your situation. He will respond to anyone's bold step of faith. Remember, Peter was a man with human shortcomings that we all have to deal with. Unfortunately for Peter, his shortcomings were on display for all of us to read about. They were placed in Scripture, not to shame Peter, but to show no matter who you are or what you have done, you too can know and see God's power work through your life. You are never too far from God's powerful, lovingkindness and grace. All things are possible for those who believe!

Prayer

Heavenly Father, I come on bended knee and ask that Your authority and power be released through my prayer. Therefore, I command in Jesus' name that this situation be removed from my life and that provision, healing, and deliverance invade this need and overwhelm it with Your resurrection life. Death cannot stand before Your glory, so I ask You to show me Your glory, and let Your light and power expel this darkness from my life. In Jesus' name. Amen.

Declaration

This situation I'm facing is not an end. It is not marked by the finality of death. No, this situation is for the purpose of seeing the victorious power of Jesus Christ being made evident in my life. I refuse death and embrace Your resurrection life. I know that to proclaim life to this situation gives You joy, and I believe my joy will be fulfilled as well. Thank You, my Lord. I praise You in advance for the victory. In Jesus' name.

> *In that day you will no longer ask Me anything. Truly, truly, I tell you, whatever you ask the Father in My name, He will give you. Until now you have not asked for anything in My name. Ask and you will receive, so that your joy may be complete* (John 16:23, 24).

Day 28

Spare Change to Heaven's Riches

It's time to raise your expectations, for God has exceedingly, abundantly more to offer you than you can ask or think.

The Paralyzed Man at the Gate Beautiful

> *One afternoon Peter and John were going up to the temple at the hour of prayer, the ninth hour. And a man who was lame from birth was being carried to the temple gate called Beautiful, where he was put every day to beg from those entering the temple courts. When he saw Peter and John about to enter the temple, he asked them for money. Peter looked directly at him, as did John. "Look at us!" said Peter. So the man gave them his attention, expecting to receive something from them. But Peter said, "Silver or gold I do not have, but what I have I give you: In the name of Jesus Christ of Nazareth, get up and walk!"*

Taking him by the right hand, Peter helped him up, and at once the man's feet and ankles were strengthened. He sprang to his feet and began to walk. Then he went with them into the temple courts, walking and leaping and praising God.
When all the people saw him walking and praising God, they recognized him as the man who used to sit begging at the Beautiful Gate of the temple, and they were filled with wonder and amazement at what had happened to him. While the man clung to Peter and John, all the people were astonished and ran to them in the walkway called Solomon's Colonnade. When Peter saw this, he addressed the people: "Men of Israel, why are you surprised by this? Why do you stare at us as if by our own power or godliness we had made this man walk?

The God of Abraham, Isaac, and Jacob, the God of our fathers, has glorified His servant Jesus. You handed Him over and rejected Him before Pilate, even though he had decided to release Him. You rejected the Holy and Righteous One and

> *asked that a murderer be released to you. You killed the Author of life, but God raised Him from the dead, and we are witnesses of the fact.*
> *By faith in the name of Jesus, this man whom you see and know has been made strong. It is Jesus' name and the faith that comes through Him that has given him this complete healing in your presence* (Acts 3:1-15).

In this testimony, we read of a man in his forties who was born with a crippling ailment that left him unable to walk his entire life. He had never known a single day of what it would be like to walk or run, let alone, just being able to stand on his feet.

His daily routine was to have people, probably family members bring him to his spot at one of the twelve gates to the temple that was once in Jerusalem. He would sit all day on his little mat probably in all kinds of weather begging for any act of charity from those who were entering the temple grounds. He had to because this was the way he eked out a living in his very small world, sitting on his very small mat. Who knows how gifted he was and what his story might have been had he not been dealt this horrible hand at birth? How demeaning it must have been to have to beg for money and praise those who gave him some of their spare change.

It makes me wonder how many times Jesus and His disciples would have walked by this man as he asked them for alms. Surely, he must have heard about all the miracles Jesus was doing. Why did he not reach out to the Lord? Was it because after all those years he no longer had any hope that his condition could change? Maybe he reasoned that this was his lot in life and focused his energy on just making enough to get by. One can only speculate on such things, but I know of no instance where the Lord refused the request of a son or daughter of Abraham for healing. In fact, he couldn't even refuse the plea of faith from a non-Jew, even when it was not yet their time to hear about Jesus as the redeemer for all mankind.

James wrote in his self-titled epistle on the subject of prayer, "You do not have because you do not ask" (James 4:2). He then goes on to say that when you do ask, you ask for the wrong things. What if every time the Lord came near this man, he only asked for money? What if every time he asked the Lord for money, Jesus gave him some of what he asked for? If that were true, how tragic it would have been that he would have set his sights so low in asking for the Lord's help. If he had gotten his health back, he could have begun to work and aim to achieve his goals and dreams. All of these scenarios are merely speculation; the good news was that everything was about to change for this man. He may have long forgotten about Jesus, but Jesus had not forgotten about Him.

As Peter and John were about to go through the gate called Beautiful, the beggar called out to them for any money they could spare. The apostles' money pouches might have been empty, but their hearts were full of the riches of heaven. They walked up to the man and told him to focus on them. I wonder if he thought in his mind, "This is a busy time of the day. I have no time for small talk. What if someone rich goes by?" Nevertheless, he set his attention on Peter and John, and they gave him his healing in Jesus' name.

Peter spoke words of faith to him, and before he could finish processing what Peter had said or what was happening, he was grabbed by the hand and lifted to his feet. That is pure faith in action done in an intercessory fashion; that man experienced the faith of another on his behalf. I would guess that the presence of the Lord was so strong on him, he had a feeling something extraordinary was going on, which would have also ignited his faith to believe.

Immediately, Peter and John knew that God's power was released, and they pulled him up onto his feet. As they did that, the man's ankles underwent a miraculous transformation, and his body responded to God's healing power. He had to learn how to walk, and he took those first wonderful steps of freedom.

Can you picture in your mind the joy and celebration that would have taken place in that man's heart? It was a day that changed his life forever. Sometimes, God will give you what you want and let you stay in it until you're finally ready to ask Him for change in your life. It was just another day for that man until God offered him something better.

When the amazed crowds recognized the man, they asked how this could have happened. Peter replied by saying to them,

> *Why do you stare at us as if by our own power or godliness we had made this man walk?* (Acts 3:12).

He then told them,

> *By faith in the name of Jesus, this man whom you see and know has been made strong. It is Jesus' name and the faith that comes through Him*

> *that has given him this complete healing in your presence* (Acts 3:16).

That healing occurred, not because Peter or John was so holy. Rather, it happened because they had faith in their Savior, as well as the power and authority given in His name. It was not just belief that was needed to see that miracle because belief is a generic form of coming to the knowledge that something is true. We live in belief every day of our lives, for we know that there will be a sunrise whether we see it or not. We know that water quenches thirst; food satisfies hunger, and so on. But to see the miraculous is to have our beliefs infused with belief in Jesus and the power of His name. That transformation of belief is called faith. It is like changing the amperage and power cord to handle the connection to a greater power source.

The power cord of a lamp in your home cannot sustain the power required to operate an electric range. It requires a heavy duty stove plug to handle the higher amperage necessary to run the appliance. Faith is the rewiring of your ability to receive from God. It is like having the proper heavy gauge power cord returned to your life enabling you (like the oven) to operate at its full potential. God never designed man to function without being connected to Him.

Jesus restored the connection to God, and it is through our faith in Him that our power cord is transformed and restored to its original design.

Let us intertwine our lives completely with His life, so we can always access his power in every need that should ever arise. Let us no longer operate our oven of creative power with the power of a child's toy – "Easy Bake Oven" with its lamp cord and a light bulb for its operation. God has so much more for our lives. It is His good pleasure and desire to display His power in and through us.

In terms of value, what was that healing worth to that man? He was given a new life through that healing miracle. He could walk and have what everyone else took for granted. If we take the costs of surgery in our day and the revolutionary new prosthetics that are available, the costs may well take us into the hundreds of thousands of dollars. This man was given a gift that was priceless, and it was delivered to him in the name of Jesus.

It's Time for Great Expectations

Maybe you're in a similar situation where your hope for health and healing is now but a faint whisper. There have been too many negative medical reports and too few reasons to hope. The medications have not brought any real change, so you have settled into a mindset that you are just running out the clock and wondering when it will all end.

Well, these testimonies of healing are here to tell you that it does not have to be the case. It's time to raise your expectations. You might be thinking to yourself, "I don't see any great healer or holy man knocking on my door and bringing me some reason to hope." But on the contrary, hope has come by the mere fact that you're reading this book. You don't need some great man of God to pull you to your feet as if that was the reason you could be made well. Remember, when everyone got excited over what they thought Peter and John had done, Peter said, *"Why do you stare at us as if by our own power or godliness we had made this man walk?"* He told everyone that the man was healed because of faith in the name of Jesus.

It had only been a few short weeks prior to this man's healing that Peter had denied he even knew Jesus. Think of how low he must have felt about himself; yet, God used him for a mighty miracle to be displayed in the city of Jerusalem.

Friend, it is always about Jesus, it's not about who we are or how we measure up. It is about His love for us. I promise you, He has not forgotten you. In fact, a priceless gift from the Lord is waiting for you, and it is released by faith in the all-powerful name of Jesus.

Let this book be as Peter was to that man, and let God's Word complete its desired mission for your healing.

Prayer

Heavenly Father, in Jesus' name, come and meet me where I am. Manifest Your miraculous healing power. Help me to hope again, and raise my expectations to believe You for the miraculous. I ask that I would be made completely whole because I too believe and have faith in the name of Jesus. Amen.

Declaration

Jesus, I believe You love me as much as You loved that person who was healed in this story. I believe You are the same person now as when You walked this earth two thousand years ago. I believe You hear my prayers, and now, it is my time to experience the miraculous. I declare that Jesus is all I need to be made well and in the name of Jesus, I believe I have been made completely whole. Thank You for my miracle, for I believe in the power of Your mighty name. Thank You, Jesus. You truly are my healer.

> *Now to Him who is able to do infinitely more than all we ask or imagine, according to His power that is at work within us, to Him be the glory in the church and in Christ Jesus throughout all generations, forever and ever. Amen* (Ephesians 3:20, 21).

Day 29

Paul's Bold Act of Faith

Sometimes, it takes a bold act of faith by someone else to initiate the faith that is already deposited in the heart of a person in need. The apostle Paul became that person for a man in Lystra.

The Healing of a Man Born Crippled in His Feet

> Now at Lystra there was a man sitting who could not use his feet. He was crippled from birth and had never walked. He listened to Paul speaking. And Paul, looking intently at him and seeing that he had faith to be made well, said in a loud voice, "Stand upright on your feet." And he sprang up and began walking. And when the crowds saw what Paul had done, they lifted up their voices, saying in Lycaonian, "The gods have come down to us in the likeness of men!"
>
> Barnabas they called Zeus, and Paul they called Hermes, because he was the chief speaker. The priest of Zeus,

whose temple was just outside the city, brought bulls and wreaths to the city gates, hoping to offer a sacrifice along with the crowds.
But when the apostles Barnabas and Paul found out about this, they tore their clothes and rushed into the crowd, shouting, "Men, why are you doing this? We too are only men, human like you. We are bringing you good news that you should turn from these worthless things to the living God, who made heaven and earth and sea and everything in them. In past generations, He let all nations go their own way. Yet He has not left Himself without testimony to His goodness: He gives you rain from heaven and fruitful seasons, filling your hearts with food and gladness." Even with these words, Paul and Barnabas could hardly stop the crowds from sacrificing to them (Acts 14:8-18).

In the ancient world, a miracle could have given you the acclaim of being a god who came to the earth. By the same token, criticizing one of the Greek gods was a sure-fire way to get killed by stoning. This is how Paul's day in Lystra almost brought his life to an end.

I See That You See

Paul was preaching to a crowd that had gathered telling them the good news about Jesus and that He was present to heal. It was then that Paul set his eyes on a man who had been listening intently to every word he had spoken. What did Paul see in the eyes of the man crippled from birth? What did the man hear from Paul's words that quickened faith in him for his healing?

That physically challenged man heard the message about the goodness of God, which would have been completely foreign to those ancient Greeks. He listened to Paul tell of the love of Jesus and how He came to save and heal the broken. When Jesus walked this earth, He quoted the first part of Isaiah 61 as His declared mandate to humanity. It reads,

> *The Spirit of the Sovereign Lord is on me, because the Lord has anointed me to proclaim good news to the poor.*
> *He has sent me to bind up the brokenhearted, to proclaim freedom for the captives and release from darkness for the prisoners, to proclaim the year of the Lord's favor* (Isaiah 61:1).

That man was hearing about a God who cared about his well-being. The gods of Greece and Rome, which he grew up believing in, were generally disinterested in people. And if they did take an interest in you, it might be to make sport of your life and mess with you. That is why offerings were made to the gods. It was to appease them and curry favor with them, so you might live a peaceful life. This man was hearing things foreign to his understanding, and a revolution was taking place in his heart and mind. His belief went from a hope that the words he was hearing were true, to a belief that God loved him and wanted him to be whole in this life.

As Paul kept glancing over at the man, he could see in his eyes that hope was forming into faith. The man's body language was bursting with anticipation that his wretched life of suffering could be changed by this one named Jesus. It may well have been that Paul looked over and saw that the man was beginning to be restless as he kept listening to his words. He wanted to do something; he had to do something. He just couldn't sit there any longer. That is when Paul moved toward him and almost shouted at him to get up on his feet. In an immediate response to Paul's command, the man who never walked a day in his life felt power in his feet, transforming his bones, sinew, skin, and tissue, and he stood up. The crowds had never seen a miracle before; hence, they thought they were in the presence of a god. They wanted to worship Paul. The ancient inhabitants of Lystra had just witnessed the power of God, and they did not know how to process that miracle.

The Bible teaches that faith comes by hearing the Word of God. That dear man sat through Paul's proclamation of Jesus. He took the grace of God for healing into his heart and made it his own. He simply believed and received; the rest was up to God.
So then, let's bring this into the here and now. You don't have to grow up in church, measure up to someone's view of being holy or somehow earn some form of righteous merit badge to be healed. The example that we learn from this man was that he heard the good news about Jesus and believed. His belief took him to a place he might have only dreamed about. When he acted on Paul's command, faith caused a transfer from heaven to earth that initiated a release of God's mighty power. Remember, just prior to his encounter with Paul, he was probably like everyone else in Lystra and was a worshiper of pagan gods. God is no respecter of persons, but He is a respecter of faith. It says a lot to the Lord when you place your hopes and trust in a God you

can't see; that greatly pleases the Lord. The man saw the kingdom of God in power that day. He saw it first, with the eyes of faith.

In this day and age, it is very easy to dismiss the miraculous as being impossible. In our minds, we reason these things away and treat these discussions as mere religious superstition, but Jesus said, *"With God all things are possible."* It didn't take that man years of study to build up his faith for a miracle; it only took action on the belief that was growing in him by the moment. He acted on his faith when Paul told him to stand up and before his mind could understand what was happening; he was healed. Make Paul's command to that man yours; it's your time to rise up and be healed!

Prayer

Heavenly Father, help me to place my heart and mind on Your lovingkindness and tender mercy. Give me the strength to take my eyes off of my current needs and problems. Open my eyes to see You in Your glory as my healer. Lord, give me a hunger to know You and Your Word so that it will awaken faith within me and cause me to step out of my circumstances. Thank You for hearing my prayer. You do hear, and I will see. In Jesus' name I pray. Amen.

Declaration

Jesus, I believe Your Word is true, and it is living and alive for me today. You said that if I believe, nothing is out of the realm of possibility for me. Therefore, I declare myself healed and my body made whole. Every cell, organ, bone, sinew, and tissue must respond to the healing power of Jesus. I command this body of mine to rise and be healed in Jesus' name.

> *The apostles performed many signs and wonders among the people, and with one accord the believers gathered together in Solomon's Colonnade. Although the people regarded them highly, no one else dared to join them. Yet more and more believers were brought to the Lord—large numbers of both men and women.*
> *As a result, people brought the sick into the streets and laid them on cots and mats, so that at least Peter's shadow might fall on some of them as he passed by. Crowds also gathered from the towns around Jerusalem, bringing the sick and those tormented by unclean spirits, and all of them were healed* (Acts 5:12-16).

Day 30

All Things Do Work Together for Good for Those Who Love God

When your ship has sailed right into the teeth of a storm and has left you shipwrecked, don't give up. God is there with you to redeem the situation. This is Paul the apostle's story of how God took something that seemed hopeless and turned it into a victory.

Paul's Shipwreck at Malta

Once we were safely ashore, we learned that the island was called Malta. The islanders showed us extraordinary kindness. They kindled a fire and welcomed all of us because it was raining and cold. Paul gathered a bundle of sticks, and as he laid them on the fire, a viper, driven out by the heat, fastened itself to his hand. When the islanders saw the creature hanging from his hand, they said to one another, "Surely this man is a murderer. Although he was saved from the sea, Justice has not

allowed him to live." But Paul shook the creature off into the fire and suffered no ill effects. The islanders were expecting him to swell up or suddenly drop dead. But after waiting a long time and seeing nothing unusual happen to him, they changed their minds and said he was a god.
Nearby stood an estate belonging to the Publius, the chief official of the island. He welcomed us and entertained us hospitably for three days. The father of Publius was sick in bed, suffering from fever and dysentery. Paul went in to see him, and after praying and placing his hands on him, he healed the man. After this had happened, the rest of the sick on the island came and were cured as well (Acts 28:1-9).

When it seems that things have gone off the rails, be ready and alert, for you are a candidate for a miracle. Your heavenly Father will use the worst the Devil had planned for you and, in turn, crush him with it. Then, with a mighty display of the power of God, He will bless you and get you to where you need to go.

All Things Do Work Together for Good for Those Who Love God

Faith Is the Buoy That Keeps Your Head above Water

Paul and the 275 people who set sail for Italy encountered the storm of storms. For two weeks, they had tried to break free of the storm but to no avail. It had been a perilous journey, and it seemed there was little to no hope that everyone on board would be able to survive. But before the shipwreck, an angel had appeared to Paul and assured him that although the ship would be lost, all of the passengers and crew would be saved. Their ship was broken in two on a sandbar near shore. Those who could swim did so, and those who could not clung to the debris of the ship and waded to shore. All would make it safely to shore on the island of Malta.

Paul and everyone who survived that ordeal were just hoping to find some warm shelter and get dry. They had just spent a considerable amount of time in the sea but on land, the rain continued to pour. To make matters worse, while Paul was collecting some sticks and driftwood to make a fire, a viper bit him and fastened itself onto his hand. He was definitely not having a very good day. The island's inhabitants viewed all this as justice from the gods against what must have been a very evil man.

It was only then that things began to turn around for him. Through all of those troubles, Paul remained undaunted in his faith in God. I am reminded of the words he wrote in an earlier letter to the Christians in Rome,

> *And we know that God works all things together for the good of those who love Him, who are called according to His purpose* (Romans 8:28)

When the people realized he was not swelling up and dying from the snake's venom, things immediately changed. They had never witnessed anyone survive a viper's poisonous bite before, so they changed their minds and believed that he must have been a god. Paul was then brought to the governor's father who was ailing with dysentery. After Paul prayed for him, he immediately recovered. That healing triggered a revival as all of Malta's sick and afflicted came to Paul to be healed. In the end, a disaster was turned into a victory that led to most of the island's inhabitants being converted to Christianity. Paul went from being shipwrecked on Malta to receiving Malta as his prize to offer to the Lord.

We live in a fallen world and being a Christian is not an exemption from the challenges that come in this life. However, we are promised that God will be with us in our times of trouble and see us through to a victorious end. Believers have a tendency to want to put halos on the Christians we read about in the Bible. We want to venerate them as heroes of the faith and put them on pedestals because of their exploits. There is no question their calling was great, and their faithfulness to the Lord is worthy of high praise, but at the end of the day they were people just like you and me. They had to walk out their faith in the Lord through the trials of this life in the same way we have to.

Many times in Paul's letters, you will read that he was in despair because of the difficulties he faced. He had to encourage himself in God, pick himself up and press on. No matter who you are or how great the calling, we all have to walk in faith, and it is made alive in all of us the same way. It comes through the living written Word of God, the Holy Spirit speaking to us, as well as through the encouragement of others. None of us are exempted from the walk of faith. The challenges we face become the classroom of apprenticeship to experience the power of God. No matter how bad the situation looks, your faith in Jesus can turn it around for the good. Nothing is so sweet as the taste of God turning your shipwrecked situation into a victory for you and a glory to Him.

Prayer

Father, forgive me if I have bemoaned my situation and through despair have wanted to give up the fight. Stir up my heart through Your Word that I would rise up in faith and believe it is not the end, but rather, the turning point to victory. Fill me with boldness to believe and declare Your words of hope and life that I may see it through to the fulfillment of my prayers. In Jesus' name.

Declaration

No matter the challenge, adversity or the disappointments, I will not quit. I will see the power of God deliver me through every difficulty because He is faithful and true. God is my provider and healer. He is my all in all, and I declare that I will trust Him. I will see His goodness and mercy overtake me and bring me to the shores of His victory. In Jesus' name, I stand on the firm, dry ground of His promises and believe that I have what I declare. In Jesus' name. So be it.

> *And God was performing extraordinary miracles by the hands of Paul, so that even handkerchiefs*

or aprons from his skin were brought to the ailing, and the diseases departed from them, and the evil spirits left (Acts 19:11,12).

Day 31

The Intercession of the Ministry

Every church or gathering of believers should be a well of healing for their communities. They should have a vibrant prayer ministry that serves the people entrusted to them by the Lord. Healing should be a living testimony of the local church as it continues the Lord's ministry on the earth.

Anointing Oil and the Prayer of Faith

> *Is any one of you suffering? He should pray. Is anyone cheerful? He should sing praises. Is any one of you sick? He should call the elders of the church to pray over him and anoint him with oil in the name of the Lord. And the prayer offered in faith will restore the one who is sick. The Lord will raise him up. If he has sinned, he will be forgiven. Therefore confess your sins to each other and pray for each other so that you may be healed. The prayer of a righteous man has great power to prevail. Elijah was a man just like*

> *us. He prayed earnestly that it would not rain, and it did not rain on the land for three and a half years. Again he prayed, and the heavens gave rain, and the earth yielded its crops* (James 5:13-18).

Every church that names Jesus Christ as Lord and Savior should be a place of prayer where the works of Jesus are still being manifested in our day. Unfortunately, that is not entirely the case, so it may take a little searching to find one in your city. It is in the assembly of believers where we can draw on the collective ministry of intercession to cover the needs of the church and the greater needs of our communities. James was the leader of the early church in Jerusalem, and through his letter we read and get a sense of the priorities of that church.

The believers had a practice of anointing the sick with oil as a symbolic gesture that healing was being released to the person being prayed for. We have been reading about the numerous ways Jesus healed people, but anointing a person with oil was not one of them. However, we do see the Lord giving instruction to His disciples to do so as we read in Mark's Gospel,

> *So they went out and preached that the people should repent. They also*

> *drove out many demons and healed many of the sick, anointing them with oil* (Mark 6:12, 13).

Furthermore, the parable of the Good Samaritan presents a strong image of oil being used to treat wounds.

> *But when a Samaritan on a journey came upon him, he looked at him and had compassion. He went to him and bandaged his wounds, pouring on oil and wine. Then he put him on his own animal, brought him to an inn, and took care of him* (Luke 10:33, 34).

Olive oil was used as a healing ointment in the ancient world. Hence, the Lord had His disciples use that symbolism to visualize that healing was flowing. That strong mental association made for a good contact point in believing for someone to be healed. When you couple anointing with oil and the laying on of hands by the leaders within a congregation, it completes the picture of the Lord's ministry to a person. Out of His life flows the healing oil through His words and through His touch.

When you think of someone praying for you, it seems like such a weak second option compared to the Lord Himself being there and praying for you, but actually, it's not. The Lord has given His Holy Spirit to be with His church and to empower His people. In fact, Jesus said,

> *Truly, truly, I tell you, whoever believes in Me will also do the works that I am doing. He will do even greater things than these, because I am going to the Father* (John 14:12).

Paul the apostle wrote,

> *And if the Spirit of Him who raised Jesus from the dead lives in you, He who raised Christ Jesus from the dead will also give life to your mortal bodies through His Spirit, who dwells within you* (Romans 8:11).

The same Holy Spirit that raised Christ from the dead is now indwelling His church today. If we truly believe what that means even to the smallest measure, this world would explode with demonstrations of Spirit and power. We would see a move of God on every continent and nation.

James finished his thought in this passage we read earlier by saying that Elijah was an ordinary guy who did extraordinary things. If he could do it, then so can you. You might be thinking, "I'm not righteous enough to see my prayers answered like that." The reality is no one can attain righteousness in and of themselves or through their own works of piety. James understood this, for righteousness is a gift given by God through Christ and His finished work on the cross. Righteousness cannot be earned; it is a gift. So be bold like Elijah and let your faith loose.

I encourage you to connect with a local church and allow their prayer team to minister to you; it will be a blessing to you if you do. James did not write that the prayer of faith might heal the sick; he stated that the prayer of faith will restore the sick to health.

Prayer

Lord, lead and guide me to a church that worships You as Lord and Savior and believes Your Bible as the Word of God. Reveal to me where Christians who believe in miracles and pray for the sick gather. In Jesus' name I pray.

Declaration

Lord, You said in Your Word that Elijah was a common man. Yet, You manifested Your power through His prayer. I make this my declaration that God is no respecter of persons. If Elijah can see the demonstration of Your power, then so can I. I speak Your life and power into my every need and believe that my prayers are answered. In Jesus' name.

> *But I will restore your health and heal your wounds, declares the LORD* (Jeremiah 30:17a).
>
> *Jesus Christ is the same yesterday and today and forever* (Hebrews 13:8).

This ends the devotional section of this book. I want you to know that our team has agreed in prayer that all who read this book will receive their healing from the Lord. We bless you in Jesus' name and release His power to affect healing and a cure for your body. Amen.

31 Days of Healing

Supplemental Teachings on Faith

Faith Part 1

The Difference between Faith and Belief

In terms of the language of the New Testament, there is vast difference between faith and belief. On the one hand, they seem entirely the same and operate on all of the essential principles. However, on the other hand, they part company when it comes to application and inspiration.

Belief is the confidence you have acquired through knowledge and experience that uphold the opinions and imaginations of your heart and mind. For instance, you know that during the day, even when the clouds block the sun from view, the sun is still there. You know from experience that your chair will support your weight and that food will satisfy your hunger. Those beliefs are so completely embedded in your soul that you do those things on a daily basis without even a thought or consideration to question your actions.

But even beyond what is seen in the here and now, belief can affect those things that have not yet happened. At the heart of self-help teaching and sports psychology is the process of visualization and actualization. Athletes now rehearse the game in their minds before playing them, visualizing their moves on the field or the shots they take on goal and where they directed those shots.

I remember a poll that was conducted a few years back at all NHL training camps where they asked every player to give a percentage in relation to how much of the game preparation was mental and physical. The poll numbers that returned were as high as 90% for mental preparation. It wasn't skating, passing and shooting drills that made them into elite athletes. It was their ability to slow the game down in their mind, believe in their capability to perform and execute that success in their minds over and over again. For many athletes, this visual game preparation, self-belief, and confidence is as important to their game as any physical preparation would be nearing the time given to it, nearly as much as physical practice. Self-help coaches and teachers use actualization methods to redirect what a person believes about him or herself, by forming a positive structure of self-confidence, leading the person to a belief in his or her own capabilities to succeed.

All of these programs and practices place the focus and attention on the individual with no required spiritual input. Therein lies the greatest difference between belief and faith; it is here where those paths part company. Faith is more that just a noun used to describe a religious belief or tenet; it is belief that enjoins itself with a trust in God to infuse your belief with His power. It is not self- reliant but God-reliant, in that you deem God more faithful to meet your need than you can. Generally, that is not the case in life as people go about and carry on their lives with little regard for their Creator. All of that changes when the crises of life come. They find that the things they trusted in, as well as their ability to overcome problems are of no avail. It is in those times that people turn their attention to God.

It neither has to be that way nor should it be because it is God's heart to be fully engaged in the lives of His children. He is not a helicopter parent hovering over your every decision imposing His will on you. Rather, He is like a loving father teaching you life skills and letting you be an apprentice with His works, so you have the wherewithal from a solid foundation to make right choices and good decisions. Just as parents would have joy in seeing their children make good decisions, so too is your heavenly Father pleased as He sees you honor the heritage He has given you. That is why it is so important to always stay in relationship with the Lord. It is through those times of knowing His presence in prayer and through His Word that you have a firm foundation to weather any storm that may come your way.

The flip side of this, (not staying in close relationship with God or the absence of a relationship with Him) is that when trouble comes you panic, not knowing what to do. The storm has come, and you have consumed all of your self-provisions; the cupboards are now bare. But even in the midst of those desperate times, God is never farther than an honest prayer away. His storehouse is always full, and He never lacks the wherewithal to meet the needs of any heart that would cry out to Him.

You may be reading these words and questioning whether you think in the terms I just conveyed to you. I feel and write this way because over the years, I have sought to plant His words into my heart and abide in Him, which always leads to a bountiful harvest of faith. It gives me plenty of provision for my daily needs and an abundance in store to meet any future needs of others and myself.

It may surprise you to know that the word "belief" is not used in the New Testament. Only faith is used because it is a belief that is never absent of God in the context of belief. Conversely, there is no word called, "unfaith," because if God is not part of the belief, it was never faith in the first place. Therefore, there is no such word as unfaith; it is always called unbelief. Now, when belief or faith are acted upon, they both transition into believe and believing. This moves them from being nouns used to describe something, to verbs, which are now something in motion. It is through the energy of motion that things happen. Belief is powered by human energy and faith is powered by God. So how do we engage our faith and make it effectual?

Faith, Hope, and Love

> *And now these three remain: faith, hope, and love; but the greatest of these is love* (1 Corinthians 13:13).

These three words are the essence of how God's kingdom operates, and all play an intricate role in seeing what we are believing for come to pass. We seem to be always looking for the key formula to achieve success, but with God, it all comes down to relationship. Faith, hope, and love are three words that are the foundation of any great and lasting union. In fact, it is from the root of the word faith that we get the word faithfulness, which is comprised of fidelity, devotion and loyalty. Treachery is its opposite meaning. Its implication is to break faith with someone and thereby violate that loyalty. Without fidelity and loyalty, the relationship is built and housed on shifting sand and is scarcely able to withstand the slightest storm. So then, we see through this imagery that faith is not a formula; rather, it is about trust. It is trusting that God is loyal, faithful, and His fidelity to you is without question. His heart never changes toward you. We may be unfaithful, but He remains ever faithful. This is what Paul wrote concerning the faithfulness of God,

> *This is a trustworthy saying: If we died with Him, we will also live with Him; if we endure, we will also reign with Him; if we deny Him, He will also deny us; if we are faithless, He remains faithful, for He cannot deny Himself*
> (2 Timothy 2:11-13).

The bottom line of faith is the knowledge that God is impassioned in His love for you and can be trusted with your heart and life. Your best interests will be at the center of His every thought toward you.

From this perspective, you can see how hope and love come into play in this context of relationship. People in love lower their defenses, become vulnerable, and reveal their hopes and dreams believing they will be embraced and shared together. Faith pleases God because it is a mutual trust of love to share the journey together.

> *And without faith it is impossible to please God, because anyone who approaches Him must believe that He exists and that He rewards those who earnestly seek Him* (Hebrews 11:6).

Another form of imagery is used to describe the harmony of faith, hope, and love that brings the desired result. I have put together some well-known verses to form some thoughts:

> *But what does it say? "The word is near you, in your mouth and in your heart," that is, the word of faith we are proclaiming: that if you confess with your mouth, "Jesus is Lord," and believe in your heart that God raised Him from the dead, you will be saved. For with your heart you believe and are justified, and with your mouth you confess and are saved* (Romans 10:8-10).

For the word of God is living and active. Sharper than any double-edged sword, it pierces even to dividing soul and spirit, joints and marrow. It judges the thoughts and intentions of the heart (Hebrews 4:12).

The book of Revelation describes the Lord in his glory like this, *He held in His right hand seven stars, and a sharp double-edged sword came from His mouth* (Revelation 1:16).

As they were walking back in the morning, they saw the fig tree withered from its roots. 21 Peter remembered it and said, "Look, Rabbi! The fig tree You cursed has withered."
"Have faith in God," Jesus said to them. "Truly I tell you that if anyone says to this mountain, 'Be lifted up and thrown into the sea,' and has no doubt in his heart but believes that it will happen, it will be done for him. Therefore I tell you, whatever you ask in prayer, believe that you have received it, and it will be yours (Mark 11:20-24).

Have you noticed the connection between all the things we have discussed thus far? We can see that what we say and declare becomes the initiation of action to our faith, much like turning on the ignition to your car. The Word of God is like a powerful weapon at our disposal. When spoken over our situations, it cuts through anything we face. Jesus is symbolically revealed as having a sword in His mouth, which indicates the power of His words. We are created in the image of God and can wield the sword of faith-spoken words with the authority given by Jesus in the Word of God. Jesus said that anyone could speak to the mountain, so you are within your right to replace the word "anyone" with your name.

Since Jesus used a weapon of His day to describe the power of believed words, I will use a more modern weapon to show the same symbolism. Your mouth is like that of a loaded firearm. Your tongue is the trigger, which through your words of faith unleashes its power. Hope is like the shell cartridge that provides the platform to carry the payload or projectile, which is the munition of faith. Without a combustible material to launch the munition, the shell casing and projectile remains dormant. It needs a propellant or gunpowder, which is love that fires the projectile of faith to overturn and destroy the attack of the Enemy against your life.

> *This is why the Son of God was revealed, to destroy the works of the devil* (1 John 3:8b).

Your faith in God is released by your words that were initiated through hope and works through love. Notice the combination in play in the following verse,

> *For through the Spirit, by **faith**, we eagerly await the **hope** of righteousness.*
> *For in Christ Jesus neither circumcision nor uncircumcision has any power, but only **faith** working through **love*** (Galatians 5:5, 6).

Love was at the heart of everything the Lord persevered and overcame in order to redeem mankind. Every spiritual battle, all that He suffered in soul and body was out of His passionate love to end the enmity between God and man. He made peace through His cross to restore the relationship between us and to empower us by faith to announce that good news to the world.

When love is the motivating factor in all that you do, can any prayer of faith fall short of its target? The answer would be – no.

Faith Part 2

Being Fully Persuaded

The Bible calls Abraham the spiritual father of all those who have faith. In an age where people worshiped idols made by the hands of men, Abraham with a simple childlike trust, believed in the unseen God of heaven. As God made Himself known to him, he walked in faith by following the Lord's plan for his life in spite of the lack of physical evidence. It is from this brief examination of the example he set for us that we can understand his honorary title.

> *Against all hope, Abraham in hope believed and so became the father of many nations, just as he had been told, "So shall your offspring be." Without weakening in his faith, he acknowledged the decrepitness of his body (since he was about a hundred years old) and the lifelessness of Sarah's womb.* **Yet he did not waver through disbelief in the promise of God, but was strengthened in his faith and gave glory to God, being fully persuaded that God was able to do what He had promised.** *That is why*

> *"it was credited to him as righteousness."*
> *Now the words "it was credited to him" were written not only for Abraham, but also for us, to whom righteousness will be credited—for us who believe in Him who raised Jesus our Lord from the dead. He was delivered over to death for our trespasses and was raised to life for our justification* (Romans 4:18-25).

Abraham was an extraordinary individual and is the noted example of a man of faith. He grew up in a land with numerous idols that were worshiped as gods, but he pressed past all the religions of his day and worshiped the God of heaven. He chose the unseen realm over the religions of a seen world with its idols made of stone, wood, and metal. The more he experienced this unseen God, the more he was persuaded of God's faithfulness. That belief in the unseen realm brought about angelic visitations and prophetic dreams and encounters into Abraham's natural realm. He had no guidebook or template, only a scant, oral, tribal history to work from. Yet, from that posture of faith, he pursued the God his ancestors spoke about.

It is one thing to be persuaded about something but another thing to be fully persuaded like Abraham was. When you are almost persuaded that something is true, there is still plenty of room for anxiety or hesitancy to influence your beliefs. You move about slowly and exercise extreme caution when you are uncertain of your surroundings or the situation you are in. It is like stepping out on a small frozen lake wondering if it is solid enough to support your weight. It is only after you are fully assured that the ice is thick enough that you lace up the skates and start to play some "Shinny," which is the name for pond hockey. How do we become fully assured of the promises God has given to us from His Word?

The more time you spent on the surface of that ice, the more experiential knowledge you were gaining about its ability to support your weight. As you moved further out on that lake, a transformation was taking place. Any fear of breaking through the ice was lessened to the point that you knew it would not happen. This is the illustration of how our faith in God grows stronger over time. We experience His goodness, learn of His lovingkindness toward us and it creates a boldness and confidence in our knowledge of Him. That was one of the goals of this book, to bring you to a place where you are fully persuaded that God's promises are true and that they are true for you. In reading and meditating on these daily testimonies of God's goodness and power, it is my belief that God's Word will become so real to you that you will speak to any mountain you face, and it will obey you, just as Jesus said it would.

Watch the words you speak and believe about yourself, for there is power in believed words. As much as positive words bring about results, negative words work the same way. Think about the challenges a person who has been dealing with a condition over a long period of time would face. If it is a chronic illness, it will have even longer negative effects; thus making it harder for the person to have hope that a miraculous change will happen. To break through this, you have to change your thoughts, which will affect your belief. When that belief is centered in God, it will eventually be expressed through your words and actions.

What if there is no time to gain the experience of a life with God, which can produce that confident trust in Him? Does that mean there is no hope for someone who needs a miracle right now? Absolutely not, if that were the case, few would ever receive their miracles. Also remember, you're not alone in this because God shares the same desire for your well-being as you do. He has an unending reservoir of His grace for us, and it truly gives Him pleasure to release all of the benefits of His kingdom to us.

Think about what life was like for the man written about in John's Gospel who was born blind. He didn't even know who Jesus was; yet, he still received his healing from the Lord. Everyone who knew this man couldn't believe he was the blind guy who begged at that gate daily. His world changed after one brief encounter with the Lord on what otherwise would have been just another day. Jesus loves you no less than He loved that man. He is the living expression of every promise in the Bible for us today.

Each devotional told a story of people in desperate circumstances who exhibited everything from no faith, to great faith and everything in between. The difference for every person in need was Jesus. He was their X-factor, and He is your X-factor today.

Faith in Action

Faith is a belief in God that leads to an action, which originated from a hope you held in your heart. That hope transitioned to faith when you believed something that had not yet materialized was a reality. When your heart is persuaded that what you believe has to manifest in the physical realm, it will begin to govern your actions and bring them in harmony with your faith. When this conviction of faith rules over your words and actions, it engages God's power.

God created the universe by envisioning what He wanted to do and was convinced that it would materialize according to His mighty power as He spoke it into being. The molecular structure of the universe came together and is held together by the word of His power. It is your heavenly Father's desire to empower your words in the same way. That's what Dads do; they want to pass on their knowledge and experience to their children. The Lord wants to empower your words that are in agreement with His will. Be certain of this: healing is His will.

> *Consequently, faith comes by hearing, and hearing by the word of Christ* (Romans 10:17).

As we have discussed earlier, faith is formed by hearing God's Word and believing it in our hearts. It does not come by merely reading words on a page; it comes by owning those words you read and believing them in your heart.

Faith and the Anti-Faith – Fear

I am sure you have read, heard or seen films that depict the antichrist as the incarnate of evil who is bent on establishing his evil empire and imposing great suffering and loss upon humanity. The word "antichrist" literally means from the Greek language, "one who sets himself up alongside and opposes Christ." In other words, one who sets up a shadow kingdom (in this case, a dark shadow) to mimic and oppose the kingdom of Christ. So, if the kingdom of darkness is a mere shadow kingdom then it would stand to reason that it would have similar workings to its power. As we have already discussed, faith accesses the power of God; therefore, in like manner, fear can unwittingly access the power of evil.

It was Franklin Delano Roosevelt who said in his inauguration speech in 1932, "The only thing we have to fear is fear itself." When you think about it, there is considerable truth in that statement and here's why.

Anxiety creates scenarios in your mind of events that have not yet happened. It gathers strength as you become convinced that what has not happened will happen. It is then that fear takes hold and empowers your negative thought to take an adverse action. That action could be the paralysis of inaction that seems to short circuit your ability to think and act. None of those things have happened; yet, your life is being governed by them, leading you into a downward spiral. This is anti-faith. It is a negative counter action that works like faith.

> *For God hath not given us the spirit of fear; but of power, and of love, and of a sound mind* (2 Timothy 2:7 KJV).

When you trust in God's faithfulness, it steadies your heart and mind. It keeps you on a clear path to receive His power, so you can overcome every anxious and fearful thought and crush it with the truth from God's Word. This is the essence of spiritual warfare,

> *For though we live in the flesh, we do not wage war according to the flesh. The weapons of our warfare are not the weapons of the world. Instead, they have divine power to demolish strongholds. We tear down arguments, and every presumption set up against the knowledge of God; and we take captive every thought to make it obedient to Christ* (2 Corinthians 10:3-5).

Spiritual warfare is a battle for the hearts and minds of every man, woman, and child. Therefore, keep your heart and mind filled to overflowing with the knowledge of God.

Guard Your Faith against the Voices of Unbelief

It is truly sad that even religious beliefs can strip away any hope a person might have that God will intervene and do the miraculous in his or her life. Some religions teach that the negative things which happen in a person's life are predetermined, for it is your karma. It is simply your lot in life or you have been fated to your situation. Even in Christianity, there are those who teach that God uses sickness and disease to teach us something. If any of those scenarios were true, then why wouldn't we just surrender to the illness or disease and not fight against those important instructional lessons for our lives? Instead, we fight the illness every step of the way, with every resource available to us, because deep down in our hearts, we know these religious teachings are not true. Deep down in our spirits, we know this is not the way our lives should end, and we fight until every ounce of hope and strength is gone.

God has placed deep within our consciousness the intuitive truth that healing and health are our right. Many of us grew up reciting the Lord's Prayer that said, "Thy will be done on earth as it is in heaven." Is there any sickness or disease in heaven? Of course not! We also read,

> *If anyone confesses that Jesus is the Son of God, God abides in him, and he in God. And we have come to know and believe the love that God has for us. God is love; whoever abides in love abides in God, and God in him. In this way, love has been perfected among us, so that we may have confidence on the day of judgment;* ***for in this world we are just like Him*** (1 John 4:15-17).

If we are like Him in this world, we realize that He is not sick or diseased in heaven. So then, if Jesus is healthy and whole, should not that also be our right?

Unfortunately, the negative teachings believed by many in our day, are the seeds that produce the crops of failure. That is a harvest we never want to see taking place in our lives. We need to weed out these false teachings and accept the heart of God as expressed through Jesus in His ministry on the earth.

> *You yourselves know the declaration having come through all Judea, having begun from Galilee, after the baptism that John proclaimed: how God anointed Jesus of Nazareth with the Holy Spirit and with power, and **how Jesus went around doing good and healing all who were oppressed by the devil, because God was with Him*** (Acts 10:37,38).

Those verses summarize God's heart for them and you on the matter; nothing has changed in our day and age. Jesus is still doing good today. He is manifesting that truth through those who believe His Word and minister healing to the afflicted and oppressed.

Faith Part 3

Health and Healing Maintenance Program

This chapter will help you understand how the kingdom of God functions, how your seed of faith grows and develops, as well as how it is challenged by the Enemy in an attempt to thwart your harvest. Knowledge is power; this will help you keep and maintain what God has apportioned for you.

The Parable of the Sower

> *Once again, Jesus began to teach beside the sea, and such a large crowd gathered around Him that He got into a boat and sat in it. All the people crowded along the shore, and He taught them many things in parables.*
> *And in His teaching He said, "Listen! A farmer went out to sow his seed. As he was sowing, some seed fell along the path, and the birds came and devoured it.*
> *Other seed fell on rocky ground, where it did not have much soil. It*

sprang up quickly, because the soil was shallow. But when the sun rose, the seedlings were scorched, and they withered because they had no root.
Other seed fell among thorns, which grew up and choked the seedlings, and they yielded no crop.
Still other seed fell on good soil, where it sprouted, grew up, and produced a crop—one bearing thirtyfold, another sixtyfold, and another a hundredfold."
Then Jesus said, "He who has ears to hear, let him hear" (Mark 4:1-9).

The Parable of the Sower Explained

Then Jesus said to them, "Do you not understand this parable? Then how will you understand any of the parables?
The farmer sows the word. Some are like the seeds along the path, where the word is sown. As soon as they hear it, Satan comes and takes away the word that was sown in them. Others are like the seeds sown on rocky places. They hear the word and at once receive it with joy. But they themselves have no root, and

Faith Part 3

Health and Healing Maintenance Program

This chapter will help you understand how the kingdom of God functions, how your seed of faith grows and develops, as well as how it is challenged by the Enemy in an attempt to thwart your harvest. Knowledge is power; this will help you keep and maintain what God has apportioned for you.

The Parable of the Sower

> *Once again, Jesus began to teach beside the sea, and such a large crowd gathered around Him that He got into a boat and sat in it. All the people crowded along the shore, and He taught them many things in parables.*
> *And in His teaching He said,*
> *"Listen! A farmer went out to sow his seed. As he was sowing, some seed fell along the path, and the birds came and devoured it.*
> *Other seed fell on rocky ground, where it did not have much soil. It*

sprang up quickly, because the soil was shallow. But when the sun rose, the seedlings were scorched, and they withered because they had no root.
Other seed fell among thorns, which grew up and choked the seedlings, and they yielded no crop.
Still other seed fell on good soil, where it sprouted, grew up, and produced a crop—one bearing thirtyfold, another sixtyfold, and another a hundredfold."
Then Jesus said, "He who has ears to hear, let him hear" (Mark 4:1-9).

The Parable of the Sower Explained

Then Jesus said to them, "Do you not understand this parable? Then how will you understand any of the parables?
The farmer sows the word. Some are like the seeds along the path, where the word is sown. As soon as they hear it, Satan comes and takes away the word that was sown in them.
Others are like the seeds sown on rocky places. They hear the word and at once receive it with joy. But they themselves have no root, and

they remain for only a season. When trouble or persecution comes because of the word, they quickly fall away.
Still others are like the seeds sown among the thorns. They hear the word, but the cares of this life, the deceitfulness of wealth, and the desire for other things come in and choke the word, and it becomes unfruitful.
Yet others are like the seeds sown on good soil. They hear the word, receive it, and produce a crop—thirtyfold, sixtyfold, or a hundredfold" (Mark 4:13-20).

Jesus told His disciples that this parable of the sower was the key to unlock all of His parables. In doing so, it will unlock the mysteries of the kingdom of God. The Lord is the farmer in this parable who was sowing those seeds, which were His words of truth.

The rest of the story is about those seeds germinating, breaking through the soil and maturing and bearing fruit to harvest. A person's heart is the soil that contains all of the nutrient potential to grow anything that would be planted in it. It's not neutral, meaning that within its very nature, it provides the perfect environment for the seed to grow. The nutrients found in it and its ability to retain moisture allow the seed to begin its transformation process.

Every belief you hold in your life is a seed that can grow to its designed potential in that soil. Having said that, let's consider for a moment what are those 6 things Jesus spoke about that keep a plant from reaching its potential or hinder its growth and limit the future harvest.

The Hardened Ground

The first thing Jesus mentioned was ground that had been trampled upon such as a path or a road. The compacted soil did not allow the seed to take root and it simply remains on the road and becomes food for the birds to consume. Those seeds never had a chance to fulfill their potential from the DNA within them. Setbacks, failures, and suffered injustices in our lives are all like the path or road that has experienced the weight of many feet pressing down on it. What would otherwise be a fruitful field is something just walked upon.

Jesus alerted His listeners to the fact that when the sown seed of His Word does not get a chance to take root in your heart, Satan, your adversary, just devours it like the birds He described. He prevents any chance of that seed taking root in your life. We could spend a great deal of time contemplating on the whos and whys of what brought about the trodden circumstances in that person's life. I am sure there is help to be found in those discussions, but the primary question is, what will bring that soil back to its intended use?

After every harvest season and before the new planting, the soil has to be prepared and the fallow ground needs to be broken up. Will those who walked all over you in your life, do that for you? Of course not, that action will be done by the one who owns the field, so it begins with us. Plowing a field in the ancient world was hard work was carried out by oxen. Isn't it interesting that one of the spiritual images associated with Jesus is the symbol of the ox? The ox is a servant and typifies the heart of Jesus as the servant of God and humanity. He won't leave this difficult labor for you to do. He will carry the load and the burden, so just join yourself to His yoke. The next question we need to ask is, "How do we break up that hardened soil" in order to begin our quest for harvest?

Change Your Mind

The first thing that must be done comes at the point of belief. The first message Jesus proclaimed implored the people to change the way they think about God. He said, *"Repent for the kingdom of God is at hand."*

That word "repent" has so many harsh religious connotations attached to it; yet, its actual meaning from the Greek literally says, "to change one's mind with purpose." Jesus was telling the Jewish people who were steeped in religious traditions that they needed to change the way they thought about God and how He feels about them in order to experience the wonderful joys and blessings of His kingdom. To place this in the context of this discussion your first step is to stop allowing yourself to be trampled upon by the opinions of others. The genesis of that reality begins with how you see yourself. Stop seeing yourself as a failure, inadequate, not worthy or a victim. Start seeing yourself as God sees you, which is a person so desirable that the God of heaven seeks to have a relationship with you.

Every time you cast down those thoughts that say you are unworthy or that you deserve the hand you feel you have been dealt, you have changed how the field of your life is to be used. You are so valuable to God that you were in His very plan of redemption; you could say you were in the DNA of His humanity whom He died to redeem. Therefore, you are also a part of His resurrection to a new life in Him. Every positive statement you make that agrees with God's thoughts of love and favor for you is like taking the plow to that hard ground, breaking it up, and turning it over for seeds to be planted in it.

It all begins with believing that God's intention and plans are to bless and favor you,

> *For I know the plans I have for you," declares the LORD, "plans to prosper you and not to harm you, plans to give you hope and a future"*
> (Jeremiah 29:11).

Jesus revealed His earthly mandate when He quoted from a prophecy given by Isaiah concerning the Messiah,

> *Then Jesus came to Nazareth, where He had been brought up. As was His custom, He entered the synagogue on the Sabbath. And when He stood up to read, the scroll of the prophet Isaiah was handed to Him. Unrolling it, He found the place where it was written:*
> *"The Spirit of the Lord is on Me, because He has anointed Me to preach good news to the poor. He has sent Me to proclaim deliverance to the captives and recovery of sight to the blind, to*

> *release the oppressed, to proclaim the year of the Lord's favor." Then He rolled up the scroll, returned it to the attendant, and sat down. The eyes of everyone in the synagogue were fixed on Him, and He began by saying, "Today this Scripture is fulfilled in your hearing"* (Luke 4:16-21).

It was the Lord's mandate to minister this message to all humanity, not in word only but in power to manifest His kingdom in your life. Do you see any condemnation, judgment or wrath in His calling as Messiah? His declaration was your promise and birthright! When you let that truth set in, you have just nestled that seed into the soil of your heart. It is there that a transformation miracle begins to take root.

The Rocky Field

The second description used in this parable is that of a field that has not been cleared for farming. He uses this illustration to speak about two more key elements that hinder the harvest you are believing for. A rock-strewn field that has not been cleared creates three problems for a farmer. The first being that the usable surface area of the field is reduced due to the fact that the rocks have not been removed and cleared. This decreases the maximum potential of the field for planting and future harvests. The second threat to the growth potential of your harvest is that which lies beneath the soil. Those rocks that have not been removed are also in part or in total, lying beneath the soil and will hinder the depth of root for that planted seed. The third problem the Lord described is the difficulty that a shallow rooted plant will experience when the hot sun radiates off those rocks. He uses this picture to describe how persecution and life's troubles challenge the plant's growth and life.

The two essential elements that a plant needs for health and development are sunlight and water. God has designed your heart to be the perfect soil match for His Word to create a climate of faith, which grows the plant to a ripe and bountiful harvest. The troubles that you face in your life are like those big rocks that are strewn throughout your field. When the rains that would replenish the crops come because the seeds are not effectively absorbed into the soil, they will run off to be absorbed in the soil elsewhere.

The sun provides energy to the plants through its leaves. The plants also need the moisture provided through its roots to grow. Rocks hold and radiate heat; they quickly dry out the soil and dissipate the moisture that would otherwise be used to nourish the plant. So, how do troubles and persecutions act like that rocky field depriving that plant of its destined harvest?

In the context of this parable by Jesus, the seed is His Word. Therefore, the persecution of His words of life will come in the form of lies that resist that truth. So in light of this, the rocks are the lies and unbelief that are trying to prevent you from believing for a successful and blessed life. Remember, Jesus said that this type of heart initially receives the seed with joy, which indicates a sense of hopeful excitement for the future. However, as contrary pressures attack that joyful hope, the crop begins to wither under the heat of the troubles of life. I find it no surprise that when Jesus was being tested by the Devil as described in the Gospel of Matthew Chapter 4 that Satan tried to tempt Jesus with God's own Word. The very Word that brings life through its light was now being misused in an attempt to wither the firm belief in the Lord's heart. Since Satan also uses words to create wrong beliefs, he uses people as his medium for his propaganda. Unfortunately, these words may come from those we hold dear, and they may even quote the Bible to move you from your hope.

To further persecute your belief, you will be beset with stories of how people succumbed to the situation you are facing and did not survive. Others will urge you to lower your expectations and prepare for the worst. To yield your faith to these words of unbelief is to wither under its strain. Letting those words of fear, defeat, and loss dwell in your thoughts will lead to an erosion of your confidence and cause you to question whether your seed will ever produce a harvest. Do not let those troubling, albeit real circumstances wilt your belief, for it will be like seeing the precious replenishing rains running off a dry and thirsty soil. You may be asking, "What am I to do to prevent this from ruining my harvest of answered prayer?"

Clear the Field

Every rock is like a negative thought or belief competing to change the environment of your field. You need to clear your field of all the negativity and persevere with faith in Christ through the troublesome realities you face. As we have discussed previously, these competing thoughts need to be vigorously arrested and cast down. Your field of harvest is also your field of spiritual battle.

There is a war going on for your belief. Your Enemy wants to keep you defeated, beat down in sickness and poverty and to crush your hopes in order to prevent you from ever elevating to faith. Paul is describing this battle as a war of words and whoever triumphs over the belief wins the battle. We need to take every negative thought prisoner and no longer give it any voice to speak into our lives. It is at this crossroad that change takes place. Do as the farmers do: take those rocks that are removed from the field and use them to build a wall to keep predators out and away from your coming harvest. Make every negative thought obedient to Christ by refuting the lies and fears. Turn those negative words to your confessions of faith in God's provision and well-being for your life. Every rock cleared makes new soil available for more seed and a greater harvest.

The Unkempt Weed Infested Field

Lastly, in this parable, Jesus likens the cares of this life, the deceitfulness of riches and the lust of other things to that of an unkempt field overgrown with thorns. Every farmer knows that after the fields are cleared, the ground is broken and the seed is planted that there is still more work to be done. Now comes the daily maintenance of his field and crops to achieve the highest yield. This is the new priority through the rest of the growing season. Clearing the fields of unwanted weeds that compete for the life of the plant becomes one of constant supervision.

It should come as no surprise to us that weeds often grow faster than the plant we are seeking to grow. They quickly compete for the sunlight, moisture, and nutrients of the soil. If left unattended these worthless growths will choke the precious crop and wreak havoc in your harvest. In this parable, the first three things Jesus spoke of as it relates to threatening your harvest were mostly external in origin. The next area of attack will mostly come from within a person.

Cares or anxieties gain their strength in our thoughts through fear and seek to embed the sense of peril to our hopes and dreams. If not removed, they will form an anti-belief to your faith and will work to undermine your faith through fear. Faith and fear operate in the heart of man exactly the same way. Both begin as seeds of thought, which, like the DNA of a seed, hold its future design within it. Either seed will envision and work toward a future result that has not yet happened. As that belief intensifies in the mind and heart of a person, it leads to a corresponding responsive action. Good or bad, faith or fear, it will produce an outcome when cultivated to completion.

The "deceitfulness of riches" is a phrase Jesus used with intent. One translation uses the phrase, *"the seductiveness of riches."* How often have we heard someone say, "If I had money, all of my problems would be solved"? While the immediate crisis might be solved, the reasons that got that person in that situation in the first place have not been addressed. Therefore, the problem could very well repeat itself again and again. The Lord's desire is for to grow and mature in Him in order to retain all that He desires to bless you with. Unfortunately, quick fixes seldom offer long-term solutions. Few things in life have such a heavy choking effect as the weight and burden of financial pressure. Great marriages have buckled under its strain and duress. However, much of that stress could be avoided by adopting a more modest lifestyle. But that too is part of the trappings of riches in the perception that it will increase your happiness.

This brings us to the last of the six things Jesus warned are at war with your harvest. The lust of other things is literally the strong pressure to ingratiate the urge to want. It is not solely of a sexual nature, but any strong pressure for immediate gratification. This points to a life that has not been grounded in Christ and is easily influenced by external things that are perceived to satisfy our cravings. The fact of the matter is that lust is never satisfied; it always wants more. These competing growths will divert your focus from the true harvest you are seeking to produce and leave you with a fruitless field of unwanted growth. Pull up those weeds before they pull down your dreams of harvest.

Jesus said the kingdom of God works in the way that was described in this parable of the sower. He gave it to us as a practical template for our lives to reveal to us how to produce a successful harvest in the face of the challenges that are real and before you.

This message is the building block for growth to anyone who will take the Lord's words to heart. Yet, as you have read in this devotional, you have seen Jesus meeting individuals wherever they are at in their lives. He became their game changer. His heart abounds in mercy and compassion and will meet you in whatever shape your field is in. I have never once read where Jesus told a soul in need to go and read the parable of the sower and get back to Him. A person in need is never far from His compassion, for healing personified His ministry.

> *Jesus went around doing good and healing all who were oppressed by the devil, because God was with Him* (Acts 10:38b).

That is the way it is with God. He will give us the blueprints for success in life through His Word, but at the same time, He is never far from us. He acts sovereignly by His Spirit in our times of crises.

If we had a fuel gauge that would indicate the faith levels of the individuals from the devotional section we have read, they would vary widely. We have read of people operating from tanks that were empty, to tanks that were full and everything in between. The difference in every case is Jesus and His heart to meet them wherever they were and answer their needs. You can do nothing to void His love for you or prevent His mighty power from operating in your life.

One last thought: never adopt a sickness by giving it an entitlement. Don't own your sickness by calling it "my arthritis" or "my cancer." Treat it like it is the very enemy of God, (which it is) and regard that illness as an unwelcome squatter in your home that is about to be evicted.

It is time for your breakthrough. Faith in Jesus and His willingness to meet you at your point of need starts the countdown to the release of His mighty power.

> *As God's fellow workers, we urge you not to receive God's grace in vain. For He says: "In the time of favor I heard you, and in the day of salvation I helped you."*
> *Behold, now is the time of favor; now is the day of salvation!* (2 Corinthians 6:1, 2).

Final Thoughts

We trust that this book has been an access point to the healing power of Jesus. Keep feeding your spirit with His Word and the harvest of faith will continue to grow and multiply.

If you have not received Jesus as your Lord and Savior, please pray this simple prayer; your world will never be the same again.

Heavenly Father, I believe that Jesus is the Son of God and Redeemer of the world. I believe that Jesus paid the price on the cross for my sins. I turn my life over to You and receive Jesus as my Lord and Savior. I ask You to fill me with Your Holy Spirit and empower me to live a life that honors You. Thank You for this free gift of grace. Live Your life through me. In Jesus' name, I pray.

If you would like any additional prayer, please feel free to contact me via email at mergingstreamsmedia@gmail.com. We would be honored to join our faith with yours.

For those of you who have already received your healing and feel that this book has been a help for you in that process, please let us know. Testimonies of healing are always such a great encouragement of the Lord's continued ministry on the earth.

About the Author

T M Leszko has spent over 30 years in combined ministry and the corporate world. His current business interests are on three continents with an added focus on book writing and publishing.

He also serves as a director of the Noiva Foundation. The organization's chief purpose is to work towards a non-political solution for reconciliation between Israel and its neighboring Arab nations. In working with governments and the private sector, Noiva has found a willingness in those from both sides of the political and cultural spectrum to work towards peace in the Middle East. Noiva also shares a vibrant vision of ministry that provides aid to the less fortunate in the Middle East and Africa.

For more information about Noiva, please visit the website at *www.noiva.ch*

For more information about this book or other offerings by T M Leszko, please visit our website at *www.mergingstreamsmedia.com*

www.ingramcontent.com/pod-product-compliance
Lightning Source LLC
Chambersburg PA
CBHW020418010526
44118CB00010B/305